Fighting Temptation - The Word Way

Bryan Amit Prasad

WESTBOW®
PRESS
A DIVISION OF THOMAS NELSON
& ZONDERVAN

WestBow Press books may be ordered through booksellers or by contacting:

WestBow Press
A Division of Thomas Nelson & Zondervan
1663 Liberty Drive
Bloomington, IN 47403
www.westbowpress.com
1 (866) 928-1240

ISBN: 978-1-4908-5861-6 (sc)
ISBN: 978-1-4908-5862-3 (hc)
ISBN: 978-1-4908-5860-9 (e)

Library of Congress Control Number: 2014919542

Printed in the United States of America.

WestBow Press rev. date: 11/21/2014

Contents

Introduction

I have noticed for many years that whenever the word *temptation* is mentioned, the moods of people change. The word seems to instill fear and apprehension, since we know we all have been under its attack in one form or another.

To see preachers stay away from talking about it should not be any reason for me not to write about it by the grace of God. Jesus, our Master, said that it is a sure thing that temptation and offences will come to everyone.

You will have an opportunity to be tempted, tested, and tried; the question is what you will do when that happens. Being better prepared by the Word of God is the best defence we have against all the fiery darts of the Devil.

In this book you will learn the ways in which temptation is targeted toward us and how you can overcome it. What is the biblical way of living free from the power of temptations? God through his Word has defined for us what the Devil has been doing from the beginning in tempting humans; his ways have not changed, though his methods have evolved.

As we learn to walk and live by the prescribed way of the Master, we shall never fall when tempted. In the prayer that Jesus modeled for the disciples, he showed them how to pray, saying: "May we enter not into temptation, but deliver us from evil."

Open your heart, and let us approach this book to learn and grow strong in living a life of constant victory. May the Lord Jesus grant you the power of His Holy Spirit to meet all the evil tendencies of the flesh by been spirit led.

Dear Father, help us to watch and pray that we enter not into temptation. In Jesus' name, we pray, amen.

Grace to you.
Bryan Prasad

Dedication

I dedicate this book to all those who are seeking God for direction to overcome temptation and live free from guilt, condemnation, shame, and disobedience. Faith-righteousness is what they seek and not guilt and sin-consciousness.

CHAPTER 1

Why Study Temptation

Temptation is as old as the existence of humanity. It has not grown weak; rather, it has grown as strong as many have allowed it to become.

There was a day when a bright and shining angel, made for serving God, rebelled. He was self-lifted up in pride. Angels have the power to make a choice but not the right to make one. He did, and before he and one third of his followers could even think another thought, they were cast out of heaven.

In his anger and rage to fight back at God, which is never going to be possible, he went after the god-man. For man looked like God and had both the right and the power to make choices. The angel now had an opportunity to get even. Yet there was a problem: how could he speak to the man? Being a spirit, he needed a body.

One day he saw the man and woman's talking pet, Snaky. He promised Snaky that if he would let the angel speak to man and woman through his body, then he would make Snaky the ruler of the animal kingdom, since Snaky was the only talking creature. The offer was too good to pass by, so he agreed. Snaky was also deceived, as were the one-third of the angels that supported the Liar.

Notice that when God made Adam, He made Snaky as his friend, yet God said it was not good for man to be alone without a comparable mate. Therefore, He made the woman. You see, Snaky was not comparable to Adam.

The angel got into Snaky and started to sow doubt into Eve. He knew if he continued to question and kept up a stream of fiery thoughts against God's faithfulness, he could make them disobey God. He also knew that disobeying God's Word was sinning against God, and then God would have to judge His man. Eve finally took the bait; she started to speak the words of the deceiver speaking through Snaky. Soon she was talking to Adam night after night about why it was all right to eat. Adam began to feel the pressure to give in, and eventually he did.

With Snaky and Eve leading the way, Adam did commit what would be known as the highest form of treason. One man would make all people sinners by his one act of disobedience. The Devil rejoiced uncontrollably: plan successful, temptation executed, man defeated. Adam did not realize what he had done by giving into temptation. With Eden lost and sorrow gained, he and Eve were expelled from God's presence.

That was what the enemy of humanity desired. He was already judged and awaiting final sentence, but by this act of tempting man he bought himself six thousand years of humanity's lease on earth. He was enthroned as god of this world. People became his slaves: now he could cause God pain by using his weapon of temptation on the humans God so dearly loved. Not for the last time, temptation won by condemning people and ruling by guilt.

God always has a plan far better and greater than either people or the Devil can come up with. I call it *God's plan of redemption*. The Devil had no idea what this meant, when God spoke judgment with His promised salvation. The Devil had no idea what was in the mind of God. You see, the Devil is limited, self-blinded to spiritual knowledge. Therefore, all his tests and trials are based on what one can see and feel.

Have you ever noticed that God did not speak to the Devil when judging Adam and Eve, because the Devil was in the body of Snaky while God was passing judgment? When God came to the snake, He first dealt with Snaky: "On your belly now you shall move, and dust shall be your food." God also took away from Snaky the power of speech, splitting his tongue in two.

As for the Devil in Snaky, He said that "the seed of the woman shall destroy the Devil, and he will bruise his heel." The Devil from then went after the most important, the firstborn, so as to remove the one to destroy his power and take the authority back which he took from Adam.

Therefore, we see him tempt Cain to kill Abel and doing his best to kill Moses and Joseph. He did his best at the birth of Jesus but kept failing. God knows more than we try telling him, though it be breaking news, *He knows it all.*

In reading the Bible you will never find an incident where the Devil manifested himself to tempt people to sin in disobeying God's direct command. Yet you will notice that through thoughts, condemnation, and suggestions, the Devil has worked one person against another. That is the reason Paul reminded the believers that we are not fighting each other and that people are not our problem; the Devil is, because of his accusations. The children are not the problem, nor is the marriage partner; the Devil is the problem.

Today, every person is tempted in one way or another. Every temptation is different, and the way the enemy brings it also varies, yet his chief end is to see us stumble and fall into sin; which is come into disobedience against God's Word and plan for our lives.

For when we sin or disobey the laws that God has set up, we bring into our own self judgment. Many have this idea that when one disobeys a direct word of God, it is at that moment God judges that person or the disobedience (sin). That is not true. God has already judged sin. He has pronounced His curse on whosoever commits sin and will face its consequences. The only way we experience these consequences is by yielding to temptations instead of yielding to God and His Word. For example, if I told you that a certain tree does not have good fruits in it and you knowingly went ahead, ate from that tree, and got sick, would you blame me for the sickness, or the tree—or yourself for not heeding the warning?

It is also very important to remember that in Christ Jesus, your sins and judgments are forever gone. Mercy and grace have triumphed over judgment; yet that does not give us the liberty to break the laws of nature and God.

There is a lot of confusion in the church as to Jesus forgiving our sin. There is one and only one sin that will keep you from heaven: that is to deny Jesus and His sacrificial work on the cross for your sins. You are a sinner, not by works, but by birth, therefore a new birth is needed in your life. As Jesus said, *You must be born again.*

A born-again, Spirit-filled believer can choose between two places to live: the kingdom of God or the world. The kingdom of God is here on earth, a life led by the Holy Spirit, guided by the Word of God rather than by the world's system. This means taking firm against living by the standard set by this present evil culture of our day either through movies, television programs, or the news media.

The world is a devil-ruled system of doing things that are completely against the Word of God. This is where lust of the eyes, the lust of the flesh, and pride of life have free rein. The blessings of God are only found in the kingdom of God, but curses, sin, sickness, diseases, and poverty both spiritually and physically are found in the world.

God's judgment is already passed on sin and the world from the beginning and whoever stays in that system of the world will experience the effects of the curse. That is why God told his people in the time of Moses, at the first Passover, *Keep covered under the blood, and no devil of death can touch you or come near your dwelling.*

As you read this book, pose and ask yourself this question: which kingdom am I in?

"... But as for me ..." (Joshua 24:15)

Joshua made a choice. What about you? Ask yourself, "This sickness, this lack in my life, could it be because of my disobedience toward God's Word? Could it be that I am staying and living in a wrong system?"

God's blessings are found only in His kingdom, when we fully receive the will of the Father here on earth.

> [The Father] has delivered *and* drawn us to Himself
> out of the control *and* the dominion of darkness
> and has transferred us into the kingdom of the
> Son of His love ... (Colossians 1:13)

When God says *love*, the world says *hate*; when God says *forgive*, the world says *revenge*; when God says, "I love you," the world says, "Nobody loves you or cares about you." When God says, "I am the Lord that heals you," the world says, "We have medicine, technology; and if that fails, it's just God's will for you to go through this pain and die." God says, "I will meet your every need," yet the world says, "These are hard times; you will really have to work hard to make ends meet."

God and His Word reign supreme in God's system (His kingdom). But the Devil and his lies rule the world, *until we do something about it.*

Brethren, you should never be found in the worldly system. I am not against the world, because we all live in it, but just as the Word says, we are in the world, but not of the world. It's the system I am against, and so is God. The point that stands is that with the five physical senses we contact the system of the world, but with the spirit we touch the kingdom of God.

One may ask why it is so important to learn about temptation and how to overcome it. Temptation started with the Devil, who desired to replace God and was kicked out of heaven. You see, Adam and Eve were tempted by deception, but Satan was not deceived; he made a deliberate choice to usurp the throne of the Almighty.

Heaven was where the presence and provision of God were found. What caused the Devil to be thrown out of His presence was his own enticement and covetousness to be God.

Even since the creation of humanity, God's desire is to make a little dwelling down here on earth. The devil has come in to tempt people in order for them to fall from God's grace and be thrown out of God's presence and provision.

Now you see how Adam and Eve got thrown out of Eden, where God and His provisions were found. They yielded to the Devil's temptation instead of yielding to God, their maker and Lord.

Some say the highest form of treason was committed by Adam, yet the story does not end there. God, the Father, promised to restore humanity back to His presence and his former glory by way of the second Adam (Jesus). Thank the Lord for his restoration in our life.

Adam's sin was so great that only atonement could restrain God from fully showing his wrath and judgments on the acts of disobedience (sin). Therefore, only one exactly born like Adam, who had God as his father, could eternally purchase, through his life sacrifice, and pay the full penalty of sin's work in our lives. It's only through the blood of Jesus that we who are born of Adam are restored back to the presence of God, our Father.

> Well then, as one man's trespass [one man's false step and falling away led] to condemnation for all men, so one Man's act of righteousness [leads] to acquittal *and* right standing with God and life for all men.
>
> For just as by one man's disobedience (failing to hear, heedlessness, and carelessness) the many were constituted sinners, so by one Man's obedience the many will be constituted righteous (made acceptable to God, brought into right standing with Him). (Romans 5:18–19)

Never ever cease to thank God for the blood of Jesus. It's our only connection back to our Father's Presence. All the Promises and blessings of God have their foundation for a believer in the power of the blood of Jesus.

I shared this with you to show you where it all started: at the garden, at the Tree of Knowledge of Good and Evil when Eve and Adam were tempted. God has not changed, and neither has the Devil; he is still using his weapon of temptation to get the believers cast away from God's presence, His provision, and His fellowship.

Praise God for His Word that teaches us what to do and how to overcome these temptations.

> Blessed (happy, to be envied) is the man who is patient under trial *and* stands up under temptation, for when he has stood the test *and* been approved, he will receive [the victor's] crown of life which God has promised to those who love Him. (James 1:12)

This is the best reason why we should understand temptations: know that temptation will surely come, but if I stand patiently and overcome it, I shall receive a *crown of life* as a reward from God. The best part is that God has promised it, and He will never break His promise.

Many believers are very afraid of tests and trials of life and wish if possible to avoid them or some other way not to go through them. Yet when you examine the Bible, you notice that David had to go through trials; Daniel and his three Hebrew friends had to; the apostle Paul had to; and even (or especially) Jesus had to go through testing. The lesson is, when encountering trials, just go through them, since God has promised to be there and strengthen us, keep us from the fiery furnace, even keep us from being drowned through shipwrecks. Jesus said He will *never* leave you helpless. Take comfort, and praise the Lord for His Love.

Tests, trials, and temptations reveal our faith and expose where our allegiance lies. They reveal what we really are and what we really believe. One can never get pure gold until it is put through the fire. In the fire the gold does not diminish in quantity or quality, but rather it is purified and made better.

> So that [the genuineness] of your faith may be tested, [your faith] which is infinitely more

precious than the perishable gold which is tested *and* purified by fire. [This proving of your faith is intended] to redound to [your] praise and glory and honor when Jesus Christ (the Messiah, the Anointed One) is revealed. (1 Peter 1:7)

Think of it as walking up to God in heaven and personally receiving from Him the crown of life. We may never be rewarded here on earth, never be recognized for our efforts and hard work. But if we have overcome temptations which test our faith and obedience to God and his Word, God guarantees us a reward.

> I know your affliction *and* distress *and* pressing trouble and your poverty—but you are rich! and how you are abused *and* reviled *and* slandered by those who say they are Jews and are not, but are a synagogue of Satan.
>
> Fear nothing that you are about to suffer. [Dismiss your dread and your fears!] Behold, the Devil is indeed about to throw some of you into prison, that you may be tested *and* proved *and* critically appraised, and for ten days you will have affliction. Be loyally faithful unto death [even if you must die for it], and I will give you the crown of life. (Revelation 2:9–10)

Here again, in the letters to the churches, Jesus mentions a *crown of life* for those in the church who keep strong and hold to their faith in Jesus, even facing death. Our declared faith in Jesus as Lord and Savior of the world must never bow to interfaith compromises.

What we believe is in the Bible, and forsaking all, we follow the Master and Lord Jesus.

Most believers somehow come to think that we shall never have any kind of suffering but instead walk through a bed of roses all the time. But that is a wrong idea. I understand we don't have to suffer any sickness, for Jesus took those stripes for our healing; we don't have to suffer lack, for He became poor that we may be enriched. What I am talking about is suffering as a believer: being ill spoken of by your own family, wrongly abused in the workplace because you are a believer in Jesus who chooses to do the right thing, even when the opposite is required. There are many places to this day where believing in Jesus is like choosing death at the hands of society, families, and even the government.

It's for the sake of your faith in Jesus and His Word (principles) that is put on trial that you have to suffer. Let me give you one scripture to make you see the importance of suffering for the faith (or rather being put through the trial of faith). For I am not ashamed of Jesus because Jesus was never ashamed of me, and never will be.

> It was then disclosed to them that the services they were rendering were not meant for themselves *and* their period of time, but for you. [It is these very] things which have now already been made known plainly to you by those who preached the good news (the Gospel) to you by the [same] Holy Spirit sent from heaven. Into these things [the very] angels long to look!

> So brace up your minds; be sober (circumspect, morally alert); set your hope wholly *and* unchangeably on the grace (divine favor) that is coming to you when Jesus Christ (the Messiah) is revealed.

> [Live] as children of obedience [to God]; do not conform yourselves to the evil desires [that

governed you] in your former ignorance [when you did not know the requirements of the Gospel].

But as the One Who called you is holy, you yourselves also be holy in all your conduct *and* manner of living.

For it is written, You shall be holy, for I am holy. (1 Peter 1:12–16)

Never think that you are the only one whose faith is being tested and put under trial. It's easy to always think of yourself when put under testing and trials. Whatever you suffer as a believer for your faith in Jesus, there are others also going through the same or probably worse situations. You are not alone in this. It's not only about you, so cheer up, child of God.

Withstand him [the enemy]; be firm in faith [against his onset—rooted, established, strong, immovable, and determined], knowing that the same (identical) sufferings are appointed to your brotherhood (the whole body of [believers]) throughout the world. (1 Peter 5:9)

I have often seen an Indian person who is converted to Jesus go through persecution which may not be as easy as it is in the Western world. Perhaps their whole family will forsake them; friends and neighbors may hate them and try their best to inflict harm on them. All this and more for just believing in Jesus and becoming a believer. I know of Sadhu Sundar Singh, who was cast out of his house, and his sister-in-law poisoned his last meal just to see him die rather than follow Jesus. Out of his experience came a wonderful song, "I have decided to follow Jesus, no turning back, no turning back."

I have been always encouraged by Paul's words in 2 Timothy:

> Take [with me] your share of the hardships *and*
> suffering [which you are called to endure] as a good
> (first-class) soldier of Christ Jesus. (2 Timothy 2:3)

So, believer, no matter how tough the going is or how hard-hitting the trial of your faith may be, go through your valley of death strong in faith. Jesus is leading the way; His Word is your lamp and light. And as you patiently endure this momentary pain, you are promised by God Almighty the crown of life as your final reward. David once wrote, "Though I walk through the valley of the shadow of death ..." (see Psalm 23). You too, as the child of the Most High, just walk though. Don't think of building a permanent dwelling in the valley of death; just pass through.

CHAPTER 2

The Temptation of Adam and Jesus

It is indeed very important to get a clear and in-depth picture of how temptation began, why some fell, and how others overcame. There is no better place to see this than in Adam and Jesus. Both were tempted by Satan, and both went through the same test, though the methods used were different. Where Adam failed, Jesus succeeded, praise God.

Many may think that Adam was not tempted; Eve was. Note, however, that God did not come on the scene looking for Eve. He said, "Adam, where art thou?!" Man (Adam) had to give an account to God for the treason, not woman. As God has taken responsibility for fallen humanity, it's time for men in every house to take responsibility for their actions toward their wife and children. God would not have accounted sin if only Eve had eaten, since then Adam only would have to forgive Eve and cast that tempter the Devil eternally from planet earth once and for all. Eve was deceived, but Adam (man in charge) walked into sin with both eyes open.

> And it was not Adam who was deceived, but [the] woman who was deceived *and* deluded and fell into transgression. (1 Timothy 2:14)

I will say something that might feel hard to take in, but you will not be able to prove otherwise: When Eve was deceived,

I believe, Adam was responsible for correcting the lie of the serpent and put things right straight away. The principle is, don't keep important issues on hold; they need attention as soon as possible. Jesus, on the other hand, came forgiving sins, and people asked, "Who is he, who forgives sin?" He was the second Adam; He had as much right, on the basis of a right given by the Father, as Adam did.

Just a glance at this opening scene of creation clearly reflects the end of the dispensation of innocence, where man has taken the backseat of complacency and compromise; and left all to the woman's hands to run the show. I hear the Lord say, "Will the real man please stand up?" Stand up for truth, stand up for his family, stand up for his children—stand up for his God.

In other words, *take charge*. It's time that you know who is responsible for the house. It's time to know where your children really are. The greatest truth of overcoming family temptations is knowing your position and taking that responsibility of resting in the favor and on the finished work of Christ Jesus.

Therefore, when Eve was deceived, so was Adam. Man, I encourage you not to just stand by and watch ongoing disobedience in your house, while you think you are trying to keep peace and love in the home. As a man, stand up for the truth of God's Word whether anyone in your house likes it or not. It's about God being pleased with you and blessing your wife and children. Your fight for truth will protect the children and family in the days to come. For certain you may not be the perfect husband or perfect father, yet the grace for fatherhood is on you to lead and guide your family in the ways of God.

Adam missed that, instead of hiding from God, he should have been seeking God's face for answers. This is where it all begins: you seek the answers for your life and family from God in prayer. Paul encourages men in the Thessalonian church to pray, lifting holy hands in faith and intercession for their own lives and families.

Now let's go back to the garden of Eden and see what is going on in this temptation.

> Now the serpent was more subtle *and* crafty than any living creature of the field which the Lord God had made. And he [Satan] said to the woman, Can it really be that God has said, You shall not eat from every tree of the garden?
>
> And the woman said to the serpent, We may eat the fruit from the trees of the garden,
>
> Except the fruit from the tree which is in the middle of the garden. God has said, You shall not eat of it, neither shall you touch it, lest you die.
>
> But the serpent said to the woman, You shall not surely die,
>
> For God knows that in the day you eat of it your eyes will be opened, and you will be like God, knowing the difference between good and evil *and* blessing and calamity.
>
> And when the woman saw that the tree was good (suitable, pleasant) for food, and that it was delightful to look at, and a tree to be desired in order to make one wise, she took of its fruit and ate; and she gave some also to her husband, and he ate.
>
> Then the eyes of them both were opened, and they knew that they were naked; and they sewed fig

leaves together and made themselves apron like girdles.   .

And they heard the sound of the Lord God walking in the garden in the cool of the day, and Adam and his wife hid themselves from the presence of the Lord God among the trees of the garden.

But the Lord God called to Adam and said to him, Where are you?

He said, I heard the sound of You [walking] in the garden, and I was afraid because I was naked; and I hid myself.

And He said, Who told you that you were naked? Have you eaten of the tree of which I commanded you that you should not eat?

And the man said, The woman whom You gave to be with me—she gave me [fruit] from the tree, and I ate. (Genesis 3:1–12)

I interject just a thought here: Could it be that Adam and Eve didn't eat immediately when the Devil spoke doubt and confusion into Eve, concerning God's Word not being true? She says in verse 3, "But of the tree that is in the middle of the garden...." I don't think she was at the Tree of Knowledge when the Devil tempted her, because they knew it was an out-of-bounds area. Verse 6 shows us that Eve went and saw. Also supporting the point that they were away from the tree is her observation about the tree "in the middle of the garden."

Eve had the hardest night sleeping due to the seed of doubt that was sown by the Devil. Reason was born to doubt God's Word. Sense knowledge was awakening to overtake revelation knowledge. The flesh was about to rebel against the Spirit of God. Death was crawling toward the human race, silencing the force of life.

Here is a provocative point for you to think about. Just as we have pets and favorites from the animal kingdom, Adam and Eve had their pet, the serpent, which talked and so could come close enough to suggest that kind of a thought to Eve. You remember when God said that it was not good for man to be alone without his kind; the serpent was not man's kind, though it was there as a pet full-time.

Yet you must also know the serpent that was with Eve was not Satan. It was only when the Devil spoke to the serpent and borrowed his body to possess and tempt Eve that they (Adam and Eve) yielded to Satan as had the serpent. The Devil must have lied to the serpent to make it the head of the animal kingdom and rule, just as he caused one third of the angels in heaven to yield to him as if they were going to overthrow God. Before responding, first read the following passage of Scripture:

> Do not continue offering or yielding your bodily members [and faculties] to sin as instruments (tools) of wickedness. But offer *and* yield yourselves to God as though you have been raised from the dead to [perpetual] life, and your bodily members [and faculties] to God, presenting them as implements of righteousness ....

> Do you not know that if you continually surrender yourselves to anyone to do his will, you are the slaves of him whom you obey, whether that be to sin, which leads to death, or to obedience which leads to righteousness (right doing and right standing with God)? (Romans 6:13, 16)

By surrendering to the serpent possessed by the devil, the lord of the earth, Adam, to become a servant to the illegal alien Satan. He became the illegitimate father of the sin-born human race. As Jesus said, you are of your father the devil who is a liar and the father of all liars, from the beginning.

Therefore God asked only Adam and Eve the reason for their disobedience, He only punished the serpent for yielding to the Devil, merely cursing him to the dust and splitting his tongue, costing him the power to speak. *Don't yield to the Devil; yield to Jesus.*

To doubt God is to have two minds on particular issues—to be double-minded as James puts it (see James 1:8). Herein is the deception: with one thought we would like to agree, and then with another we stand aloof. If you will think it, there is a 90 percent chance you will want to do it and a 95 percent chance you will end up carrying out the thought into deed.

We have so long practiced yielding to our thoughts that it has become our habit to do just what we think. Humanity has stopped living in response to the spirit in favor of mind-controlled living in the flesh.

Is there now any wonder why the devil injected reasons to block humanity from the blessing of God in our Lord and Savior, Jesus?

> Only it must be in faith that he asks with no wavering (no hesitating, no doubting). For the one who wavers (hesitates, doubts) is like the billowing surge out at sea that is blown hither *and* thither and tossed by the wind.
>
> For truly, let not such a person imagine that he will receive anything [he asks for] from the Lord,

[For being as he is] a man of two minds (hesitating,
dubious, irresolute), [he is] unstable *and* unreliable
and uncertain about everything [he thinks, feels,
decides]. (James 1:6–8)

Think about it: how is sin committed, a thought is injected by the
Devil (doubt) against what God's Word says; when we allow that
thought to live in our mind, we reason to see whether it could
be so, and this leads to a great desire to find out—or rather, to
satisfy that thought. For it is true that with the heart we believe,
but with the mind we reason. Reasons upon reasons have been
the problem where the body has been losing all battles. I think!
I wish! I don't know!

You must remember here that the only sin that will keep you
from God the father is rejecting the work of Jesus on your
behalf on the Cross. The sins we are discussing here are our
disobediences as the children of God and missing out from the
best in life that God has promised all who believe. Don't live the
life of the prodigal's elder brother, who had everything at his
disposal and yet kept himself in inferiority and missed out on
all the goodness of the father.

But every person is tempted when he is drawn
away, enticed *and* baited by his own evil desire
(lust, passions).

Then the evil desire, when it has conceived, gives
birth to sin, and sin, when it is fully matured,
brings forth death. (James 1:14–15)

The next day Eve could not wait to take Adam to that tree since
it was all she talked about that night. (God has given women
the gift of influence, but when it is used for self-gratification
and control, this is the sin of witchcraft, forcing people to do
something beyond or against their will.) They stood at the Tree

of Knowledge of Good and Evil, still pondering whether or not to partake (see Genesis 3:6).

I. They saw the tree was good for food. God gave them all other trees for food. Even though the Tree of Life was not forbidden for them to eat, yet that is what the enemy of your life focuses on, to touch what, for our own good, we are not to touch. The Word of God clearly defines the will of God, and the Devil is on constant watch to make us go against it. Now these two people were reasoning that this tree had good qualities too. In order to satisfy the lust of the eyes, they were looking for a legal way to disobey God.

II. It was pleasant to the eyes. There was nothing that seemed wrong in doing this. Faith in God and His Word does not reason out how or why; it believes and does what the Word says without questions. True faith in God's Word ends reason's reign in us. Trust does require unanswered questions in life.

III. The tree was desirable to make one wise. This is not only desire, but greed and selfishness. This is where the unsaved flesh takes its life from. (It's about me, what I like, nobody cares for me, a little sip would not hurt anybody, etc.) The flesh prompts thoughts such as this: God is withholding things from me, for I do not measure up to His demands. There is only one demand: Jesus in you, heaven inside you, as Lord of your life.

The very moment Adam and Eve ate the fruit and disobeyed God, they ceased living in the Spirit-filled, Spirit-led life, and the flesh became lord and took over, while the human spirit died and the human link to the spirit world was broken.

Verse 3 says they died—not physically, but spiritually. They were disconnected from God, their life source. As much as a fish needs water to live, so do humans need Almighty God.

Now people were eternally separated from their Creator and could never again call God their Father. No wonder that throughout the entire Old Testament God is referred to as Lord and people as servants, fallen from grace of being God's children. The apostle John, writing by the Holy Spirit, says:

> But to as many as did receive *and* welcome Him, He gave the authority (power, privilege, right) to become the children of God, that is, to those who believe in (adhere to, trust in, and rely on) His name .... (John 1:12)

The Jews had great problems understanding this. How could this Jesus call himself the Son of God, since all they knew was that they were all servants of God. However, after Jesus' baptism,

> The Holy Spirit descended upon Him in bodily form like a dove, and a voice came from heaven, *saying*, You are My Son, My Beloved! In You I am well pleased *and* find delight! (Luke 3:22)

God had not called anyone Son since Adam fell into sin. Yet God said this about Jesus since there was not a trace of sin in Him; He was born without sin. First Adam was born right till he sinned; the second Adam was also born, lived right, and opened the door of salvation for lost humanity. No wonder, as we read in John, chapter 3, we humans need to be born again from death into life. Humanity was born into the very life of God and, through the loss of fellowship, had died till Jesus, the second Adam, made available for all people a new life of God from death.

We were born naturally, in Adam, as sinners: in sin did my mother give birth to me. However, by believing in Jesus and receiving him as our Lord and forgiver of our sins, we are born again, but this time it's inside: our dead spirit is made alive. After our spirit has been made alive, we reconnect with our God and Father in heaven. We can now call him Father because of what Jesus has made available for us through His lifeblood on the cross.

When the Devil heard God speak from heaven, saying Jesus was His Son, this confused him, since he had never heard God call anyone His Son after the garden experience.

> And the tempter came and said to Him, If You are God's Son, command these stones to be made [loaves of] bread.
>
> But He replied, It has been written, Man shall not live *and* be upheld *and* sustained by bread alone, but by every word that comes forth from the mouth of God.
>
> Then the Devil took Him into the holy city and placed Him on a turret (pinnacle, gable) of the temple sanctuary.
>
> And he said to Him, If You are the Son of God, throw Yourself down; for it is written, He will give His angels charge over you, and they will bear you up on their hands, lest you strike your foot against a stone.
>
> Jesus said to him, On the other hand, it is written also, You shall not tempt, test thoroughly, *or* try exceedingly the Lord your God. (Matthew 4:3–7)

The devil saw and knew the authority that Adam had as God's son. That authority was operating in Jesus, who had come on the scene after 4000 years. Now the Devil was curious to see the same power and authority of Adam displayed in Jesus.

Whatever Jesus did and said, Adam had the same power and ability to do and perform before the fall. Today Jesus has restored to humanity that same authority and power of Adam in the garden.

The man had such powers delegated to him by God that he could forgive sins. If Eve had eaten from the tree and Adam found out, he could have forgiven the woman and banished the Devil from planet Earth once and for all.

You also see Jesus on a Sabbath day says to a lame man your sins be forgiven you and the elders questioned who He was who dared to forgive sins. The answer: He was and is the second Adam. In fact He delegated similar authority to His disciples when he said, "Whatever you bind on earth will have been bound in heaven, and whatever you release on earth will have been released in heaven" (Matthew 16:19, NET).

Now let's look at the three basic themes that the Devil used to tempt Adam and Eve.

(1) They saw that the tree was good for food.
(2) It was pleasant to the eyes.
(3) It was desirable to make one wise.

The devil masterminds these three basic considerations to cause believers to fall. He may use many other mediums and methods, but his basic aim is that we fall into sin and disobedience, by falling in these three areas.

> For all that is in the world—the lust of the flesh
> [craving for sensual gratification] and the lust of
> the eyes [greedy longings of the mind] and the
> pride of life [assurance in one's own resources
> or in the stability of earthly things]—these do
> not come from the Father but are from the world
> [itself]. (1 John 2:16)

Watch and learn carefully the demonic trend of falling into
temptation:

(1) Lust of the flesh
(2) Lust of the eyes
(3) Pride of life

After we finish studying the temptation of Jesus, we shall break
apart the three areas of Satan's rule. For now I point out that
the Devil only uses what we make available for him to use
against us. He has no outright power to tempt us unless we
draw away and entertain the lust for other things of the world
rather than seeking to satisfy our spirit and soul hunger with
the Word of God.

Keeping in mind now that sin is disobedience to God's revealed
will and command, let's look at other effects of sin (disobedience)
that followed

> Then the eyes of them both were opened, and they
> knew that they were naked; and they sewed fig
> leaves together and made themselves apronlike
> girdles. (Genesis 3:7)

Never forget that covering your nakedness will not take away
your consciousness of nakedness. Covering up sin does not take
away sin, for there is always a remembrance of it. In the same

way, atonement could only cover sin, not take it away from our conscience and restore us back the glory of God. Adam and Eve had the robe of righteousness on them. Righteousness gives you boldness to use authority and confidence to talk to God as Father and never feel inferior.

> For some little time you have ranked him lower than *and* inferior to the angels; You have crowned him with glory and honor *and set him over the works of Your hands* ..., (Hebrews 2:7)

There is only person who has reconciled us back to God. His name is Jesus, and He did it through his blood (his life).

> He went once for all into the [Holy of] Holies [of heaven], not by virtue of the blood of goats and calves [by which to make reconciliation between God and man], but His own blood, having found *and* secured a complete redemption (an everlasting release for us). (Hebrews 9:12)

Satan did not just leave Jesus once for all after the three tests; he threw his best attempts at Jesus and yet failed. Read carefully:

> And when the Devil had ended every [the complete cycle of] temptation, he [temporarily] left Him [that is, stood off from Him] until another more opportune *and* favorable time. (Luke 4:13)

The Devil does his best to bring us down through temptations; he persists in his assaults until he sees he can't win and we are unmovable in our stand of faith. Then he will go away and find other means of influencing us to fall into temptation. His major attack is through his negative, twisted thoughts, questioning the Word and love of God.

The Devil will find people to offer his temptation to divert us from God's perfect plan for our life. Yet as we go on I would like to remind you that greater is he that is in you than he that is in the world.

> And when He came to the place, He said to them,
> Pray that you may not [at all] enter into temptation.
>
> And He withdrew from them about a stone's throw
> and knelt down and prayed ... (Luke 22:40–41)

This must be one of the greatest tests and trials Jesus had to face for the salvation of humanity. He could feel the awful death of the cross, the pain, even before He went through it physically. We must remember He (Jesus) did not die as the God of the universe, but as the Son of God (the second Adam).

As He shared with His disciples, the power that lies in prayer is that those who continue to pray would overcome temptation, because prayer keeps us from even entering and yielding to temptations. For in prayer we are looking at the person of Jesus, our victory, and His Word, our comfort.

In Jesus' greatest hour of trial, look at what He is doing: praying. He did not sit around and preach a sermon, or teach and encourage anymore, or teach His disciples about His departure from them, to die and then be raised again. No! He was not doing any of these things that would likely be important in our own eyes. He refused to meditate on His troubles and fully trusted in the Father's love and mercy, which are always greater than our pain and sorrow.

Jesus would have felt the pressure from the Devil. Yet instead of dwelling on the temptation to quit, He was praying the will of His Father to come to pass. Then when Jesus was on the cross, the enemy used people to tempt Him to prove His power—just as Satan was doing when he was tempting Jesus in Luke 4. The Devil is a show-off, that's how he deceives people, with a pretense of power, keeping them in a lie and a world of deception.

> And it is no wonder, for Satan himself masquerades as an angel of light ... (2 Corinthians 11:14)

He has no light in him, but that is what deception is. The Devil does not have any love in him, so everything under his control will have the semblance, the appearance of great love and faith but it's all a pretense to hide a lie.

One cannot give what one does not have. He is darkness, and in him is no light at all.

> In the same way the chief priests, with the scribes and elders, made sport of Him, saying,
>
> He rescued others from death; Himself He cannot rescue from death. He is the King of Israel? Let Him come down from the cross now, and we will believe in *and* acknowledge *and* cleave to Him. (Matthew 27:41–42)

They were used by the Devil to challenge Jesus' desire to do the will of His Father. Satan did the same thing by entering the serpent to tempt Eve to eat from the tree that was forbidden.

Many times I have heard people complaining that God does not understand what they are going through. Let's see what the Bible says:

> Since, therefore, [these His] children share in flesh and blood [in the physical nature of human beings], He [Himself] in a similar manner partook of the same [nature], that by [going through] death

He might bring to nought *and* make of no effect him who had the power of death—that is, the Devil—

And also that He might deliver *and* completely set free all those who through the [haunting] fear of death were held in bondage throughout the whole course of their lives.

For, as we all know, He [Christ] did not take hold of angels [the fallen angels, to give them a helping and delivering hand], but He did take hold of [the fallen] descendants of Abraham [to reach out to them a helping and delivering hand].

So it is evident that it was essential that He be made like His brethren in every respect, in order that He might become a merciful (sympathetic) and faithful High Priest in the things related to God, to make atonement *and* propitiation for the people's sins.

For because He Himself [in His humanity] has suffered in being tempted (tested and tried), He is able [immediately] to run to the cry of (assist, relieve) those who are being tempted *and* tested *and* tried [and who therefore are being exposed to suffering]. (Hebrews 2:14–18)

Jesus partook of the same sufferings any human has to partake of. He felt hungry, He grew tired and rested—and He was by the way also tempted. Jesus went through everything we go through without sinning (disobedience) and without breaking any of God's promises and commands.

Now I want to take you to a passage of Scripture that will explain clearly the role of our high priest, between God and man.

> For we do not have a High Priest Who is unable to understand *and* sympathize *and* have a shared feeling with our weaknesses *and* infirmities *and* liability to the assaults of temptation, but One Who has been tempted in every respect as we are, yet without sinning.
>
> Let us then fearlessly *and* confidently *and* boldly draw near to the throne of grace (the throne of God's unmerited favor to us sinners), that we may receive mercy [for our failures] and find grace to help in good time for every need [appropriate help and well-timed help, coming just when we need it]. (Hebrews 4:15–16)

Take a moment and ponder the passage of Scripture you just read. In fact, go back and read it again. Jesus in His humanity went through all the tests and trials that all we humans face. Yet in all points He never failed; you can do the same. Greater is He, the Spirit of God, that is in you than he that is in the world.

Jesus was tempted with money, greed, pride, hate, overeating, drinking to get drunk, adultery, lust, and disobedience, yet in the midst of all these things He did not yield to temptation, nor was He overcome by any temptation. This second Adam was here to do God's will, not His own.

Though He was brought under the pressure of every temptation, Jesus pleased the Father perfectly. He never broke His word or disobeyed God's given laws and commandments.

Therefore, if anyone has the right and power to help and teach on overcoming temptation, who better than Jesus. He knows the pressure that is involved in the trial; He understands the physical pull the flesh exerts on your born-again spirit. I believe this is the reason the Bible says that *He is able* (able to help, able to give you victory over temptation) and will immediately run to the aid of one who is tempted.

You may at this point cry out, "Then why don't I overcome temptations all the time?" Read Hebrews 4:16 again:

> Let us then fearlessly *and* confidently *and* boldly draw near to the throne of grace (the throne of God's unmerited favor to us sinners), that we may receive mercy [for our failures] and find grace to help in good time for every need [appropriate help and well-timed help, coming just when we need it].

This scripture is just repeating what Jesus said before His hour of trial: "Watch and pray that you enter not into temptation."

When tempted and assaulted by the Devil's thoughts to sin against God's Word, do what Hebrew 4:16 says: *go (come) boldly into God's presence.* This is done in prayer.

You will never be victorious over temptations just by human ability or will-power. Prayer and prayer alone must meet the enemy before he enters. So we enter into God's presence in prayer, which keeps us from entering temptations. Prayer gives you a sense of God's presence, and you go through life knowing He is and you have nothing to fear; you are the righteousness of God in Christ Jesus. This sense of knowing, realized in prayer and the Word, keeps you from being drawn away by the lusts present in this world which the enemy uses against you.

For when we go before God, we receive from him *grace* and *mercy*—that's Jesus empowering Word and strength to help us overcome every test and trial and even temptations we are facing.

> He who dwells in the secret place of the Most High
> shall remain stable *and* fixed under the shadow of
> the Almighty [Whose power no foe can withstand].
>
> I will say of the Lord, He is my Refuge and my
> Fortress, my God; on Him I lean *and* rely, *and* in
> Him I [confidently] trust! (Psalm 91:1–2)

Where do you think is this hiding place of God's protection and care? It's the place of prayer, the place of total surrender to Christ's finished work and not human ability.

You cannot fight and resist the Devil in the ability of your flesh.

We must understand that the spiritual is more powerful than the physical. God who is Spirit made by His words the physical world that we know of. To tell the Devil to leave without God backing you up is a futile effort. God's Word (the Bible) is Spirit and life. Get God's Word and the promises concerning you, put them in your mouth, and speak out in faith. Through you, God is commanding the Devil to obey and leave, and he has no choice but to obey, because he hears God speaking through your mouth.

So, child of God, when faced with impossible pressures and assaulted by temptation, instead of solving it in your own ability and by human reason, go on your knees and pray. Then and only then will Jesus run to your rescue and grant you His grace (God's ability through you, though you don't deserve it). Ask Jesus to teach you in prayer how to overcome life's tests and trials and temptations, the way *Jesus would have overcome.*

CHAPTER 3

Just How Are We Tempted

> But every person is tempted when he is drawn
> away, enticed *and* baited by his own evil desire
> (lust, passions).
>
> Then the evil desire, when it has conceived, gives
> birth to sin, and sin, when it is fully matured,
> brings forth death. (James 1:14–15)

Young and new believers are usually fired up about their
newfound faith. They are very careful about everything they do
or say. They are eager to learn and spend much time at church
and in prayer groups studying the Bible, reading books, and
listening to preaching tapes and CDs. These activities usually
continue for some eight or ten months, and then comes the
drawing away, when the young saint is enticed and baited. There
is still a way to keep our fire burning by staying with the Lord
and His Word and in constant prayer.

Human nature is such that new believers are excited about
new discoveries, but as time proceeds on, the excitement starts
to fade away, and what they were so excited about and would
shout for soon becomes an old, common thing. It's not that
they don't love Jesus anymore; they do. Rather, the enemy has
succeeded in occupying their attention on other things that

seem more important than spending time with God, prayer, and Bible reading.

Believers, you must know this: the devil will not tempt you with what you don't like or desire. You cannot catch a fish with the bait that they don't even sense. You must get the right bait. I will share a little later with you how the parable of the sower and the seed is the progression of living the life Christ Jesus has called us to live.

In our flesh there dwells nothing good. Our flesh and unrenewed mind are in constant battle against the spirit-guided divine image in each of us.

Therefore, you must understand that the Devil, appealing to the flesh, works in the physical realm; God is Spirit and works in our spirit or, as we also most commonly say, our heart. God is a heart God. The devil's area of temptation will always be in the physical realm—what you see, hear, feel, touch, and taste.

So the enemy of our soul goes on to work in the areas of our weakness and presents to our flesh what feels good, smells good, tastes good, sounds good, and is attractive to behold, but guess what?. It is wrong. It's a temptation. Whenever you are tested against the Word of God, it's a devil's trap to cause you to stumble and fall. When the Word of God is sown, the enemy comes immediately to steal the Word. To repeat that, he comes to steal the *Word*.

To keep the Word from being stolen, we need to give the Word time and study for it to grow. Eve was deceived because she saw that the tree looked good, and yet by her and Adam's yielding to the temptation, sin was brought into the entire human race. That fact that something looks good does not mean is good. There is a way that seems right to a person, but it ends in destruction.

Therefore, we see here a worthy point to consider and learn: the Devil's temptations are always targeted to the physical world (the flesh).

> Therefore then, since we are surrounded by so great a cloud of witnesses [who have borne testimony to the Truth], let us strip off *and* throw aside every encumbrance (unnecessary weight) and that sin which so readily (deftly and cleverly) clings to *and* entangles us, and let us run with patient endurance *and* steady *and* active persistence the appointed course of the race that is set before us … (Hebrews 12:1)

Most of the times in our believer's walk with Christ, it's not the big sin or major trap that causes us to fall. It's those unseen, cleverly set, seemingly trivial traps that catch us unawares. Small leaks can cause more harm than we know. Let me tell you, believer, that some things that may look small could become the major cause of downfall in your growth in the Lord.

This small, insignificant thing is a trap, a temptation used by the Devil to keep you falling without you even knowing how you fell into sin again and again. Remember, there are issues in our own hearts that the Devil sees and capitalizes on. Our hearts have those unresolved desires lurking within us that we have not dealt with. They become the weapon the Devil slings back at us, trying to prove he's the one who defeats us, when it was always our heart that needed to be put right with the Spirit of God and His Word.

The Bible lets us know that it is those small foxes that spoil the vine. I have always heard believers make comments like "It doesn't matter if I drink a glass, only I must not get drunk"; "Seeing violence and murders isn't wrong as long as I don't act it out"; "It's my body, my pleasure"; and the worst one these days is this: "It doesn't matter if the person I marry is not saved now; eventually, they will get saved, after marriage."

Please answer me this: Can light and darkness be present at the same time? Can God and the Devil work hand in hand? The answers to these questions may be already given in your subconscious mind as *no!* A thousand times *no!* Yet knowing these believers are tempted by the looks and desires of the flesh to go against God's Word, to do what pleases them, and later in the marriage ceremony to kneel and ask God's blessing upon their so-called marriages. I may seem hard, but let's survey God's Word to see what He has to say.

> Do not be unequally yoked with unbelievers [do not make mismated alliances with them or come under a different yoke with them, inconsistent with your faith]. For what partnership have right living *and* right standing with standing with God with iniquity *and* lawlessness? Or how can light have fellowship with darkness?
>
> What harmony can there be between Christ and Belial [the Devil]? Or what has a believer in common with an unbeliever? (2 Corinthians 6:14–15)

Believers are not deceived when they look at the real "big picture" of life. The devil masterminds in showing believers a momentary scene and not the long-term results of this next action or word or decision.

Read Luke chapter 4 again, and then read Genesis chapter 3. You will see that when the Devil tempted Eve and Adam, he told them and showed what they wanted to hear and do. I love how one preacher defines temptation: *"When the sinful world without makes appeal to the sinful heart within, then temptation is born."*

Temptation draws power from the consent of one's own heart. Who knows how many times Eve must have questioned Adam about that tree? The Devil saw the opening and threw his seeds (thoughts) of doubt and disobedience to the authority of God's Word.

One common observation is that people do want to sin after they are born again, and if their mind is not yet renewed with the Word, they are just waiting for a reason for doing it. A poor man might always talk about the rich man being a drunkard and a womanizer, yet if he gets a million dollars, he might very well do those very same things and even worse. It's our heart's intentions that are evil, that seek an opportunity to fall into temptation.

> Search me [thoroughly], O God, and know my heart! Try me and know my thoughts!
>
> And see if there is any wicked *or* hurtful way in me, and lead me in the way everlasting. (Psalm 139:23–24)

David cried out to God to check his heart, for he knew that out of the heart flow the issues of life. Out of your heart flows forth life or death, obedience or disobedience, health or sickness. Every issue that you face comes from the heart.

It's your heart within that gives birth to temptation. Influences and enticements come pressing from the sinful world, yet it is the sinful heart that gives it the right and life to be born in your life.

> There is not [even] one thing outside a man, which by going into him can pollute *and* defile him; but the things which come out of a man are what defile him *and* make him unhallowed *and* unclean.

And He said to them, Then are you also unintelligent *and* dull *and* without understanding? Do you not discern *and* see that whatever goes into a man from the outside cannot make him unhallowed *or* unclean,

Since it does not reach *and* enter his heart, but [only his] digestive tract, and so passes on [into the place designed to receive waste]? Thus He was making *and* declaring all foods [ceremonially] clean [that is, abolishing the ceremonial distinctions of the Levitical Law].

All these evil [purposes and desires] come from within, and they make the man unclean *and* render him unhallowed. (Mark 7:15, 18-19, 23)

Now you see: don't look outside yourself to find where temptation and sin (disobedience) to God's will come from; instead, look inside. No wonder David also cried out to Jehovah to Psalm 51:10, *"Create in me a clean heart and renew a right spirit within me."*

Believers find it easy today to just blame everything on the Devil and somebody else besides themselves. Believing people need to more earnestly tend to checking out their own heart and motives before blaming their setbacks on someone else.

I agree that, when we received Jesus in our hearts and lives, we were forgiven and became the righteousness of God in Christ Jesus. But though we were baptized, the knowledge of wrong and evil desires in our life was not instantly wiped out. Didn't you read the Bible where it exhorts each of us to work out our salvation with fear and trembling (Philippians 2:12)?

Yes, we are saved not by works but by grace, yet what this passage of Scripture talks about is a little different salvation than getting saved from hell. Salvation also means deliverance, rescue, and liberation from. After being born again, we are working at our heart. The old must be replaced by new thoughts and ideas. Let's look at **Romans 12:2:**

> Do not be conformed to this world (this age), [fashioned after and adapted to its external, superficial customs], but be transformed (changed) by the [entire] renewal of your mind [by its new ideals and its new attitude], so that you may prove [for yourselves] what is the good and acceptable and perfect will of God, *even* the thing which is good and acceptable and perfect [in His sight for you].

Therein lies the "work out your salvation" principle. The church, being likened to a bride, must purify and cleanse herself for the bridegroom, and even in this work Christ Jesus helps us through His Spirit and Word. Are you willing to let the Lord Jesus do His work in you? All you must do is rest in Him, and trust that He is able. The entire renewal of our thoughts and our ways must be replaced by the views and thoughts of God's Word.

> So that He might sanctify her, having cleansed her by the washing of water with the Word ... (Ephesians 5:26)

Just how are we tempted? Ask your heart. Much is said in the Bible on the heart issue that I believe is more important to a believer than money and healing issues. For if we take care of the heart issue, the money and healing issues will be solved quite easily. Becoming a believer, as I said earlier, does not automatically take away habits and desires from your heart. The Bible teaches on crucifying the flesh and your desires and working out your deliverance. We will talk more on this in another chapter.

Let me show you a man in the Bible who was saved, who believed in Jesus, and who followed the man of God (Philip). He still found out what was in his heart, hidden down inside him, to be revealed when the opportunity showed up.

> But there was a man named Simon, who had formerly practiced magic arts in the city to the utter amazement of the Samaritan nation, claiming that he himself was an extraordinary *and* distinguished person.

> Even Simon himself believed [he adhered to, trusted in, and relied on the teaching of Philip], and after being baptized, devoted himself constantly to him. And seeing signs *and* miracles of great power which were being performed, he was utterly amazed.

> However, when Simon saw that the [Holy] Spirit was imparted through the laying on of the apostles' hands, he brought money *and* offered it to them,

> Saying, Grant me also this power *and* authority, in order that anyone on whom I place my hands may receive the Holy Spirit.

> But Peter said to him, Destruction overtake your money and you, because you imagined you could obtain the [free] gift of God with money!

> You have neither part nor lot in this matter, for your heart is all wrong in God's sight [it is not straightforward or right or true before God].

> So repent of this depravity *and* wickedness of yours and pray to the Lord that, if possible, this

contriving thought *and* purpose of your heart may be removed *and* disregarded *and* forgiven you.

For I see that you are in the gall of bitterness and in a bond forged by iniquity [to fetter souls].

And Simon answered, Pray for me [beseech the Lord, both of you], that nothing of what you have said may befall me! (Acts 8:9, 13, 18–24)

Oswald Chambers in his devotional *My Utmost for His Highest* says (September 17, emphasis added) "a man's disposition on the inside, i.e., what he possesses in his personality, determines what he is tempted by on the outside. *The temptation fits the nature of the one tempted and reveals the possibilities of the nature.*" What one is tempted by from outside is in direct relation to what is on the inside of the man. When one keeps finding a certain fault in someone all the time, really he is seeing a reflection of what he senses in himself.

Simon in the above story was doing good till he was faced with the words of the apostle: "Your heart is not right." He got saved, went to believers' gatherings, and probably gave to the work of God. Yet, though he left sorcery, the desire for power, fame, and recognition never left him.

I am saying that in the heart lie heaps of unresolved issues and wicked desires that must be dealt with by the Word of God and prayer. Just when you think you are holy and right in yourself, then something comes up in the form of temptation that causes you to fall flat on your face, without the realization where that came from. The best and easiest example of keeping your heart in check is like an antivirus program which you have to run when your computer system doesn't seem to work right because a virus has infected it.

So scan your heart every time you are faced with a temptation, because every temptation to which we fall victim is to prove whether there is still something left that must be dealt with. Don't fear temptations; most times they reveal our heart and what we are really made of. Once you catch a spiritual virus in your heart, deal with it in prayer and by the power of the blood of Jesus. Receive your forgiveness, since the Bible promises you that. Don't live with your problems—deal with them! *Mercy* always triumphs over judgment. Don't beat yourself up over the failures of your life; have faith in the faithfulness of Jesus, that He does not fail, so you will win. It is not because we are good that God is good, it is because God is good all the time that good things happen to us.

A person asked me once: After we are born again and the blood of Jesus has forgiven us of all our sins, why then do we fall short and sin as before? Wasn't the generational curse broken then? As I waited for the answer in my spirit, I was reminded of Lazarus when Jesus had called him back from the dead. He was breathing and alive but still bound by the graveclothes. Jesus said to the people to loose him and let him go.

Jesus did not loose his graveclothes; the people (pastors and leaders anointed) had to help him get loose.

> I appeal to you therefore, brethren, *and* beg of you in view of [all] the mercies of God, to make a decisive dedication of your bodies [presenting all your members and faculties] as a living sacrifice, holy (devoted, consecrated) and well pleasing to God, which is your reasonable (rational, intelligent) service *and* spiritual worship.
>
> Do not be conformed to this world (this age), [fashioned after and adapted to its external, superficial customs], but be transformed (changed)

> by the [entire] renewal of your mind [by its new
> ideals and its new attitude], so that you may prove
> [for yourselves] what is the good and acceptable
> and perfect will of God, *even* the thing which is
> good and acceptable and perfect [in His sight for
> you]. (Romans 12:1–2)

You have to do something about renewing your mind by the Word of God and prayer. It does not happen in your salvation prayer. Old thoughts must be replaced with new, godly thoughts, since thoughts play the most vital roles in our outlook and decide what we are likely to do in the future.

You will have to learn how to put on the new man and put off the old man.

> Strip yourselves of your former nature [put off
> and discard your old unrenewed self] which
> characterized your previous manner of life and
> becomes corrupt through lusts *and* desires that
> spring from delusion;
>
> And be constantly renewed in the spirit of your
> mind [having a fresh mental and spiritual attitude],
>
> And put on the new nature (the regenerate
> self) created in God's image, [Godlike] in true
> righteousness and holiness. (Ephesians 4:22–24)

"Be constantly renewed" is the message, not once for a while and then back to the old ways and thoughts. I can almost hear some crying out, "How do I do that, brother?" Then why not read on:

> Therefore, rejecting all falsity *and* being done now
> with it let everyone express the truth with his

neighbor, for we are all parts of one body *and* members one of another.

When angry, do not sin; do not ever let your wrath (your exasperation, your fury or indignation) last until the sun goes down.

Leave no [such] room *or* foothold for the Devil [give no opportunity to him].

Let the thief steal no more, but rather let him be industrious, making an honest living with his own hands, so that he may be able to give to those in need.

Let no foul *or* polluting language, *nor* evil word *nor* unwholesome *or* worthless talk [ever] come out of your mouth, but only such [speech] as is good *and* beneficial to the spiritual progress of others, as is fitting to the need *and* the occasion, that it may be a blessing *and* give grace (God's favor) to those who hear it.

And do not grieve the Holy Spirit of God [do not offend or vex or sadden Him], by Whom you were sealed (marked, branded as God's own, secured) for the day of redemption (of final deliverance through Christ from evil and the consequences of sin).

Let all bitterness and indignation *and* wrath (passion, rage, bad temper) and resentment (anger, animosity) and quarreling (brawling, clamor, contention) and slander (evil-speaking, abusive or blasphemous language) be banished from you, with all malice (spite, ill will, or baseness of any kind).

And become useful *and* helpful *and* kind to one another, tenderhearted (compassionate, understanding, loving-hearted), forgiving one another [readily and freely], as God in Christ forgave you. (Ephesians 4:25–32)

Let me list some of the things you can do to put on the new man and some things you don't do to keep the old man dead.

- ❖ Stop lying.
- ❖ Speak the truth always.
- ❖ Don't allow the Devil a foothold in any area of your life.
- ❖ Stop stealing.
- ❖ Do some honest labor.
- ❖ Give to those in need.
- ❖ Don't allow corrupt words to come out of your mouth.
- ❖ Never, ever grieve the Holy Spirit (either in thought, word, deed, or action); not walking in the righteousness that Jesus has provided is really grieving the Holy Spirit.
- ❖ Let bitterness, anger, wrath, clamor, and evil speaking be put away from you.
- ❖ Be kindhearted toward others, and forgive without recall.

We cannot believe God beyond our knowledge of His Word about matters that are important for us. As you gain knowledge of what Jesus has provided for you in the redemption, you can then walk in that provision. Today you can live healed and healthy. Jesus has provided healing for you; it's your choice whether to receive it and walk in it. The same applies to prosperity, peace, righteousness, and victory over the Devil and the flesh. Let me go one further: the blood of Jesus has the power to keep you and preserve you from living in the weakness of the flesh.

The weakness in your life that seems to constantly put you down can be totally destroyed by finding out what God has said concerning that situation. If you have a lust problem, find out what God said about lust, if you are prone to stealing, find out scriptures that deal with that topic. If you struggle with anger, go and get some anger words from the Bible. Every problem you face has an answer in the Bible.

Remember what the main aim of temptation is: to cause you to fall into sin (disobedience) and bring you under Satan's control through the false belief that "there is no way out of this." There is always a way out with Jesus. His Word gives life and strength for every human situation.

When you go to God's Word and get the truth, the lies of the Devil will be exposed. Therefore, knowing the truth brings freedom. The Word of God brings light and life and is much more powerful than any medicine or weapon.

Believers today spend *too little* time in God's Word, getting God's wisdom in their situations, and they spend *too much* time before the TV and their cell phones. Some who confess they are doing work for God really have no time for God himself.

Studying God's Word should not only be for preaching or assignments; it's your spiritual food. Yes, the Word of God is food—in fact, the most balanced diet your whole spirit, soul, and body can have. I have come to believe that if you really want any form of victory over sin, the Devil, temptation, sickness, or lack, if you don't get God's Word, you are defeated already. For God has promised to keep true not to your words, but to His own words.

How have we really fallen into temptations? And when do we make provision for the flesh!

> Clothe yourself with the Lord Jesus Christ (the Messiah), and make no provision for [indulging] the flesh [put a stop to thinking about the evil cravings of your physical nature] to [gratify its] desires (lusts). (Romans 13:14)

When you know you have a problem with overeating, don't keep buying junk snacks in your shopping. You buy and keep them in case you feel hungry at odd times, so you could munch on them. *Making provision for the flesh is simply fueling the fire to burn stronger.* You cannot fuel your body with junk and expect to be fit and fine. When you know it is dangerous to stay in the dark alone with your girlfriend or your boyfriend, then never be found alone. Meet each other where people can see you.

You are children of the light, so stay in the light. Whatever needs to be said and done, do it in the light; hiding in the dark always has some secretive intentions to it. If you get turned on by kissing and touching, then just don't. Don't make provision for the flesh to cause you to break and disobey God's Word. When you know that on Sunday you need to be in church on time, then don't go out partying all night on Saturday.

Making pro-vision is something like visualizing. You visualize drinking and you say yes to parties where you know for sure your unsaved friends will be drinking. You envision yourself going through Internet pornography, so you wait till no one's watching you or you're alone to fulfil your vision. You see yourself stealing money and go about planning how you'll do it.

Vision can and does also work for our benefit in giving us the victory over these temptations and sins when we decide to see ourselves as God wants us to see ourselves through the revealed will set in the pages of the Holy Bible. How you see yourself in Christ is the exact way the world will see you. Your inner view reflects on your outer views of yourself on others. We mostly project ourselves to others.

Whose vision are you supporting, God's, or your own fleshly one? Pro-vision is support for the vision. The question is whose. You are tempted to make provision to do wrong long before you actually do it. A man does not just get drunk one day and sleep with a harlot, having no idea how it really happened, and then blame it on the drinking.

But in reality the thoughts were there in his heart. Little by little provisions were being made, and time was being set for the fulfilment. Remember, visions are for an appointed time; though it tarries, wait for it. It will come to pass, either good or bad.

Had Samson stopped going to the Philistines to look for a wife to sleep with, his hair would have never been cut, and he would never have been defeated.

Had Jonah not foreseen and planned to run away, he would never have been swallowed by a fish.

Had David been at war rather than looking at Uriah's wife, Bathsheba, he would have never sinned in God's eyes by committing adultery and murdering her husband. He saw himself sleeping with Bathsheba, and he made provision for killing her husband and taking her in to be his unlawful wife.

> After these things, the word of the Lord came to Abram in a vision, saying, Fear not, Abram, I am your Shield, your abundant compensation, *and* your reward shall be exceedingly great.
>
> And Abram said, Lord God, what can You give me, since I am going on [from this world] childless and he who shall be the owner *and* heir of my house

> is this [steward] Eliezer of Damascus? (Genesis 15:1–2)

You will notice here that Abram, as he was called then, saw himself childless despite the promise of God Himself (see Genesis 12). He envisioned himself without a child, and that is why many believers go without the promises of God since they cannot see themselves receiving them. Look at how much God was interested in changing Abram's vision so He could give him a child.

> And he [Abram] believed in (trusted in, relied on, remained steadfast to) the Lord, and He counted it to him as righteousness (right standing with God).
>
> And He said to him, I am the [same] Lord, Who brought you out of Ur of the Chaldees to give you this land as an inheritance. (Genesis 15:6–7)

When did Abram believe? Many would say after God showed him the stars. No; instead, he could see himself with child and never again question God about a child. The stars would not let him do so. Now I will show you how this same principle proved to have become Abraham's way of life in faith. When he faced the ultimate test of his faith, it was this same pro-vision that gave him strength to *sacrifice his only son.*

Read the following scriptures carefully.

❖ The Lord's command:

> After these events, God tested *and* proved Abraham and said to him, Abraham! And he said, Here I am.
>
> [God] said, Take now your son, your only son Isaac, whom you love, and go to the region of

Moriah; and offer him there as a burnt offering upon one of the mountains of which I will tell you. (Genesis 22:1–2)

❖ Abraham's obedience

So Abraham rose early in the morning, saddled his donkey, and took two of his young men with him and his son Isaac; and he split the wood for the burnt offering, and then began the trip to the place of which God had told him. (Genesis 22:3)

❖ Abraham's faith

Abraham said, My son, God Himself will provide a lamb for the burnt offering. So the two went on together. (Genesis 22:8)

❖ Abraham's faith in action

When they came to the place of which God had told him, Abraham built an altar there; then he laid the wood in order and bound Isaac his son and laid him on the altar on the wood.

And Abraham stretched forth his hand and took hold of the knife to slay his son. (Genesis 22:9–10)

❖ God's intervention and provisions

But the Angel of the Lord called to him from heaven and said, Abraham, Abraham! He answered, Here I am.

And He said, Do not lay your hand on the lad or do anything to him; for now I know that you fear *and*

revere God, since you have not held back from Me
or begrudged giving Me your son, your only son.

Then Abraham looked up *and* glanced around,
and behold, behind him was a ram caught in a
thicket by his horns. And Abraham went and took
the ram and offered it up for a burnt offering *and*
an ascending sacrifice instead of his son! *(Genesis
22:11–13)*

❖ God's promise

In blessing I will bless you and in multiplying I
will multiply your descendants like the stars of
the heavens and like the sand on the seashore.
And your Seed (Heir) will possess the gate of His
enemies ... (Genesis 22:17)

Abraham kept speaking faith, even when he knew his son was
the sacrifice, he trusted God to keep true to His Word. Surely
God provided himself a sacrifice. Abraham knew that the Lord
has promised that in Isaac shall his descendants be blessed. If
he sacrificed Isaac then God would be lying unless God would
raise him from the dead. Let's go and get a look at Abraham's
thoughts as he went ahead to sacrifice his son.

By faith Abraham, when he was put to the test
[while the testing of his faith was still in progress],
had already brought Isaac for an offering; he who
had gladly received *and* welcomed [God's] promises
was ready to sacrifice his only son,

Of whom it was said, Through Isaac shall your
descendants be reckoned.

> For he reasoned that God was able to raise [him]
> up even from among the dead. Indeed, in the
> sense that Isaac was figuratively dead [potentially
> sacrificed], he did [actually] receive him back from
> the dead. (Hebrews 11:17–19)

Abraham had a vision of resurrection, even from the ashes. Now that is some pro-vision. He counted God and His Word faithful to perform what He had said He would. This is what God calls righteousness: he believed in what God said, and God said that is righteousness. Many say he did not do anything to get this righteousness imputed to him, but clearly he believed, and that is an action word. To believe is to act.

That is what I am saying: see yourself as dead so that the new life you live is by faith of the Son of God (see Galatians 2:20). Walk in newness of life. Yet if you keep seeing yourself falling and sinning, that is what you will be producing. Use your thoughts: pro-vision yourself free from sin, pro-vision yourself healed, pro-vision yourself blessed. Pro-vision yourself living in the overflowing, abundant life Jesus came to give you.

Ask yourself these questions when making decisions: Why are you making this decision and choice? Why do you want to do the things you are going to do? Above all, are your decisions and choices in line with what God has said in His holy Word? The main point at all times is *the intention* with which we act. If the heart's intention is wrong, then the action will be wrong.

Remember, temptation is designed to make you disobey God's Word in order to bring about God's judgment on the sin, that is, on those who disobey His Word. We are tempted when our desires for natural things are greater than for the things of God. In times like today, many are tempted to test God regarding material possessions, without which most think their life is a waste. That is a wrong vision, and such thinking has produced many strange doctrines of possession and wealth gain as a part of biblical principles.

> And they tempted God in their hearts by asking for food according to their [selfish] desire *and* appetite.
>
> Yes, they spoke against God; they said, Can God furnish [the food for] a table in the wilderness?
>
> Behold, He did smite the rock so that waters gushed out and the streams overflowed; but can He give bread also? Can He provide flesh for His people?
>
> Therefore, when the Lord heard, He was [full of] wrath; a fire was kindled against Jacob, His anger mounted up against Israel,
>
> Because in God, they believed not [they relied not on Him, they adhered not to Him], and they trusted not in His salvation (His power to save). (Psalm 78:18–22)

The lusts and desires of human beings will never say they've had enough; the more you feed them, the more they will crave.

As we have read in the preceding passages, the people of Israel tempted God for their fleshly desires. It is true, but look at it from the angle of how they were led to tempt God for the fulfilment of bodily pleasures. Time and time again believers say, "I will be satisfied if only I can have that house or that car or that mobile phone," and when they get it, for a few weeks or months they are on top of the world. Soon, however, they are crying out to God: "If only I can get *that*, I shall be happy again." *Joy and happiness are not the result of worldly gains, but are states of being—knowing who you are and who God is, and knowing God's promises concerning your every situation.*

> And time and again, they turned back *and* tempted God, provoking *and* incensing the Holy One of Israel. (Psalm 78:41)

I want you to read the following passages of Scripture *loudly and slowly* to comprehend the truth laid out for us to grasp.

> Nevertheless, God was not pleased with the great majority of them, for they were overthrown *and* strewn down along [the ground] in the wilderness.

> Now these things are examples (warnings and admonitions) for us not to desire *or* crave *or* covet *or* lust after evil *and* carnal things as they did.

> Do not be worshipers of false gods as some of them were, as it is written, The people sat down to eat and drink [the sacrifices offered to the golden calf at Horeb] and rose to sport (to dance and give way to jesting and hilarity).

> We must not gratify evil desire *and* indulge in immorality as some of them did—and twenty-three thousand [suddenly] fell *dead* in a single day!

> We should not tempt the Lord [try His patience, become a trial to Him, critically appraise Him, and exploit His goodness] as some of them did-- and were killed by poisonous serpents;

> Nor discontentedly complain as some of them did—and were put out of the way entirely by the destroyer (death).

> Now these things befell them by way of a figure
> [as an example and warning to us]; they were
> written to admonish *and* fit us for right action by
> good instruction, we in whose days the ages have
> reached their climax (their consummation and
> concluding period). (1 Corinthians 10:6–11)

We need to read the Scriptures not only for information and sermons but with a desire to do what the Bible requires of us.

Men are tempted to test God's love and mercy to fulfil their own selfish desires. Even though our desires may not seem selfish, yet what is good in our own eyes does not have to happen just because we want it to. There is a way that seems right to a man, but the end is destruction (see Proverbs 14:12).

> You are jealous *and* covet [what others have]
> and your desires go unfulfilled; [so] you become
> murderers. [To hate is to murder as far as your
> hearts are concerned.] You burn with envy *and*
> anger and are not able to obtain [the gratification,
> the contentment, and the happiness that you
> seek], so you fight and war. You do not have,
> because you do not ask.

> [Or] you do ask [God for them] and yet fail to
> receive, because you ask with wrong purpose
> and evil, selfish motives. Your intention is [when
> you get what you desire] to spend it in sensual
> pleasures. (James 4:2–3)

Many have backslidden and started working with the world just because one or two of their so-called desires and prayers were not answered. I see a trap the enemy has set when we pray. Ask yourself, "Are my prayers trying to test out God's promises toward me, or am I praying with sincerity of heart, desiring answers to benefit both me and people around me?"

There is a place where you ask in faith on the basis of what God Himself has promised you through His Word.

You can bring that before God and remind Him of His Word, for he will make His Word good. But it's a different matter to go ahead and test him by saying, "Lord, if You love me, You will give me that car. Lord, I want to know Your will concerning my future wife, but Lord, let it be Susan."

Jesus said, "If you abide in Me, and My words abide in you, ask whatever you wish, and it will be done for you" (John 15:7, ESV). That is, if His Words are in you, you are only going to ask in relation to the revealed will of God and not by what you feel and see as right in your own eyes.

I have noticed recently that believing people focus more on materializing than on the Word Himself. If you put the Word first, the material needs will be taken care of by God. Don't ever get angry at God when something you desire or prayed for has not come to pass as yet. It's not God who is at fault here. Retrace your words and prayer, find out what God said in His Word concerning that situation of yours, and pray with what God said. *When you pray the Word of God back to Him, you can be sure to get results every time.*

If you are not a giver, don't expect a financial miracle to take place, and don't blame God for your financial condition. Don't even expect healing from God by going to all the healing ministries and not to the Healer Himself. Church, it is time to honor God for who He really is—*God* Almighty and your loving Father.

I have met many believers who twist Bible verses just to do something they want to do and justify it by Scripture. Although the Bible says that we trample on serpents (Luke 10:19), that does not give us the right to start up a show where we handle poisonous snakes. We will die, and we will have no grounds to blame God's Word.

> And he said to Him, If You are the Son of God, throw Yourself down; for it is written, He will give His angels charge over you, and they will bear you up on their hands, lest you strike your foot against a stone.

> Jesus said to him, On the other hand, it is written also, You shall not tempt, test thoroughly, *or* try exceedingly the Lord your God. (Matthew 4:6–7)

Satan quoted scripture, yet he twisted it so as to tempt Jesus into doing what He did not have God's backing to do. God does not need to support a human agenda. He only supports His Word.

Child of God, get the picture here: God is God, not your genie in the jar who has to jump out and fulfill your every desire. We need Him more than He needs us. Instead of seeking our ways and desires, let's find out what are His desires and what is His will. His love for us is greater far than we will ever to able to realize.

What we see here is don't be tempted to test God or His Word for selfish desires. If you have a problem, find out, search the Scriptures to see God's mind concerning the matter. Then put your request to God in prayer, and you can expect answers. The issue today is that we don't want to spend time with God and His Word seeking answers, but that is it—the Word way to victory. I always say, *Don't strive it. Hear it!* Hearing the Word of God preached about your situations and issues will help.

I would like to drop a word here before going on. Don't continue in sin, just because you can ask forgiveness according to 1 John

1:9. Jesus said to the woman caught in adultery, "Neither do I condemn you; go, and from now on sin no more" (John 8:11, ESV). By grace you have been saved and by grace you shall continue to be saved.

Don't take an unbeliever before God for His blessings in marriage. It's not going to happen. There's no union of a believer and an unbeliever. God will not bless what He has cursed. So don't try to tempt God to do something which He says in His Word He will not do.

> But seek first the kingdom of God and his righteousness, and all these things will be added to you. (Matthew 6:33, ESV)

You will also be tempted if you walk without the knowledge of God's Word. Instead, you walk in the flesh rather than led by the Spirit of God. The Bible calls such people *simple*—those who can be easily manipulated and deceived and tempted.

Let's look at the scriptures that define them:

> How long, O simple ones [open to evil] will you love being simple? And the scoffers delight in scoffing and [self-confident] fools hate knowledge?

> For the backsliding of the simple shall slay them, and the careless ease of (self confident) fools shall destroy them. (Proverbs 1:22, 32)

> And among the simple (empty-headed and emptyhearted) ones, I perceived among the youths a young man void of good sense ... (Proverbs 7:7)

> O you simple *and* thoughtless ones ... (Proverbs 8:5)

Whoever is simple (easily led stray and wavering) ...

The foolish woman is noisy, she is simple *and* open to all forms of evil, she (willfully and recklessly) knows nothing whatever (of eternal value) (Proverbs 9:4, 13)

The simpleton believes every word he hears, but the prudent man looks *and* considers well where he is going.

A wise man suspects danger and cautiously avoids evil, but the fool bears himself insolently and is [presumptuously] confident. (Proverbs 14:15–16)

A prudent man sees the evil and hides himself, but the simple pass on and are punished [with suffering]. (Proverbs 22:3)

These verses teach us that in the kingdom of God, being simple (thoughtless, simple-hearted, empty-headed, open to evil, easily led stray to believe and do things without thinking) will be the cause of a believer's destruction. The simple can never see the dangers that lie ahead in going a certain way. Those who are wise listen to instructions and save themselves from many painful experiences.

Thoughts are wonderful ways to meditate and ponder on the goodness of almighty God. In your thoughts you can visualize the end of your actions before you ever do them. Simple people don't use their thoughts; they don't want to consider the results of what they are about to do or say. What are the consequences of saying or doing that? Visualize the end result of your actions. *Temptations will never show the end result but instead the momentary pleasure that it has to offer.*

> For the rest, brethren, whatever is true, whatever is worthy of reverence *and* is honorable *and* seemly, whatever is just, whatever is pure, whatever is lovely *and* lovable, whatever is kind *and* winsome *and* gracious, if there is any virtue *and* excellence, if there is anything worthy of praise, think on *and* weigh *and* take account of these things [fix your minds on them]. (Philippians 4:8)

Here is instruction about what we should think or meditate on. *Your greatest victory over temptation will be won or lost in the arena of your thought life.* Your meditations become your desires, your desires become your pursuit, and your pursuit becomes your character. With your character you either honor or dishonor God; nothing can be hidden from Him.

Your thoughts will greatly be affected by your eyes (what you see) and your ears (what you hear). If you desire good thoughts, watch and hear good messages.

If you put garbage in through your eyes and ears, you will have garbage thoughts.

Let's look to the Word of the Lord for instructions for the simple:

> The law of the Lord is perfect, restoring the [whole] person; the testimony of the Lord is sure, making wise the simple. (Psalm 19:7)

The Word of God from the Bible is the only thing that can help and make a simple person wise with wisdom.

> The entrance *and* unfolding of Your words give light; their unfolding gives understanding (discernment and comprehension) to the simple. (Psalm 119:130)

Would you just read that scripture again and see what the revealed and understood the Word of God can do for the simple? Putting the Word of God into your eyes and ears will replace all thoughts of anger, hatred, lust, stealing, and wickedness.

Child of God, you don't have to wait and cry out any longer for help from a man or a pastor. You got God's Word (the Bible) to start. Find all texts that cover your area of weakness. Get messages that encourage and teach you your identity in Jesus and help you understand what the finished work of Christ on the cross has provided for you.

Nothing can happen or change in your life until you get off your back, shut off that TV and computer, and start putting good faith and grace based Word of God into your life. In the times of the prophets there were only the written law and the handed-down testimony of the people of God. With that knowledge they went forward and did things in life that we today call wonders and miracles. You are in a better state than they were in, you have the message of God's Word in translation, made so easy and clear that to misunderstand means we are in ignorance.

A man once asked me, "Brother, how can I get rid of my evil thoughts?" The Spirit of God in my spirit told me to tell him this: *"Exchange them for good thoughts, for when good enters, evil has to exit."*

The same is true with faith and fear. You cannot say you have faith in God to get through and yet say you fear that it might not happen. The same is with love and hate. You cannot hate someone if you love them.

Believer, your job is to put the Word of God in your heart through your eyes, ears, and mouth by speaking it and reading and hearing it. *The Word has inherent power to produce within you the harvest of the Word you planted.*

If you plant healing scriptures (as seed), you will reap healing. If you plant love scriptures (as seed), you surely replace hate and harvest love in your life. Love of God will also overcome the spirit of lust, fear, and greed.

> My people are destroyed for lack of knowledge; because you [the priestly nation] have rejected knowledge, I will also reject you that you shall be no priest to Me; seeing you have forgotten the law of your God, I will also forget your children. (Hosea 4:6)

Believer, don't be ignorant of the whole counsel of God's Word. *Little knowledge of Scripture indeed can be very dangerous.* Believers today could have been experiencing a worldwide move of God in all denominations had they opened a little to the move of God taking place around them and supported it.

Today church leaders have become simple and thoughtless about issues like the blood of Jesus, the Ten Commandments, abortion, and injustice. They hide themselves in the comfort of their positions and never dare to walk on water. Most have no idea of the spirit world and the reality of demon possession and what to do when demons show up in a person. This is no Hollywood idea. We are called to love and set the captive free, so let's do it in Jesus' name.

God desires His body, the church, to stop to fighting and slandering each other and start praying, if they have nothing better to do. No one is better than others; we all need one another. After all, we have the same Jesus as our redeemer and the Holy Spirit as our teacher, helper, and comforter. Don't let the views of others become a hindrance to loving them; otherwise, we will use the same approach when reaching out to the lost and sinners in the world who need Jesus every second.

Don't let your simplicity stop you from walking into the full abundance of God's perfect will for health, strength, wisdom, favor, and prosperity.

Love God, and love people.

CHAPTER 4

Lust of the Flesh, Lust of the Eyes, and Pride of Life

To get a clear, biblical understanding of what these three areas of sin are and what the Bible has to say about them, we will take a Scripture-to-Scripture journey, exploring and unveiling these three weapons of the Devil to destroy believers:

- ❖ Lust of the flesh
- ❖ Lust of the eyes
- ❖ Pride of life

> For all that is in the world—the lust of the flesh [craving for sensual gratification] and the lust of the eyes [greedy longings of the mind] and the pride of life [assurance in one's own resources or in the stability of earthly things]—these do not come from the Father but are from the world [itself]. (1 John 2:16)

Sin was first introduced into the earth by these threefold temptations, and righteousness was introduced again through victory over these three temptations.

The lust of the flesh, the lust of the eyes, and pride of life live and breathe freely in the worldly kingdom (where Satan rules through the power of the flesh) but are not able to survive in the kingdom of God.

The garden was God's kingdom rule on earth. There, the Tree of Knowledge of Good and Evil represented the sense knowledge–ruled earth; the Tree of Life is Jesus.

It was not the Father's desire for us to partake of the Tree of Knowledge; we were forbidden to eat from it. Similarly today the Father forbids us from entangling ourselves with the sense knowledge–ruled worldly system or even loving anything in it to the degree where possession means more than God. Materialism is pursuing things and finding joy in the possession of things rather than in the things of God and in His Word.

Read the following verses slowly and loudly

> Do not love *or* cherish the world or the things that are in the world. If anyone loves the world, love for the Father is not in him.

> And the world passes away *and* disappears, and with it the forbidden cravings (the passionate desires, the lust) of it; but he who does the will of God and carries out His purposes in his life abides (remains) forever. (1 John 2:15, 17)

The first people in the garden lived in their bodies led by the Spirit, which was the *zoë* (life) of God in them. When they decided to satisfy the flesh, they died spiritually toward God and became alive to their sense of good and evil. The mind and human reasonings overtook authority over the body, thus subjecting to sin and as later result death, both natural and eternal.

> Once I was alive, but quite apart from *and* un-conscious of the Law. But when the commandment

came, sin lived again and I died (was sentenced by the Law to death).

And the very legal ordinance which was designed *and* intended to bring life actually proved [to mean to me] death.

For sin, seizing the opportunity *and* getting a hold on me [by taking its incentive] from the commandment, beguiled *and* entrapped *and* cheated me, and using it [as a weapon], killed me.

The Law therefore is holy, and [each] commandment is holy and just and good.

Did that which is good then prove fatal [bringing death] to me? Certainly not! It was sin, working death in me by using this good thing [as a weapon], in order that through the commandment sin might be shown up clearly to be seen, that the extreme malignity and immeasurable sinfulness of sin might plainly appear.

We know that the Law is spiritual; but I am a creature of the flesh [carnal, unspiritual], having been sold into slavery under [the control of] sin. (Romans 7:9–14)

One other area where temptation and sin took lordship and kept people in bondage is the *deeds* intended to please God and secure receive forgiveness and blessings from Him. People have a great urge to keep the law to prove their right to be heard by God. Children of God, I would like to encourage you that Jesus has already died and paid the price for you to be free from the power of the law, which is perfect and holy since it is cannot be kept, requiring the introduction of grace. It is by grace you are saved and not of works lest any should boast (see Ephesians 2:10). Today we do fulfill the intentions of the law by the law of love, empowered by the Spirit of God.

I would like to take your attention to a very important issue here that troubled Paul before he found his victory in Romans chapter 8: the issue of the flesh, which is our carnal human nature, controlled not by the Spirit of God but by our human desires. (A carnal believer is saved and forgiven of sin, yet is still in the infant stage spiritually, even after years of a believing life.) Our flesh cannot be subject to the will of God and will not be. The un-crucified flesh is always opposed and hostile to God and His Word. The flesh does not know how and has no desire to yield to the Spirit of God. That is why there is opposition toward the purposes of God.

Your flesh is your unregenerate nature, your way of doing and believing things before Jesus became Lord of your life. Another term is your *old man*. A person's soul—namely, one's will, mind, and emotions—is what houses the flesh, not the skin that covers your body. The mind of a person houses the flesh's desires and knowledge of good and evil, as well as the uncontrolled passion for fulfilling the lust of the eyes, the lust of the flesh and pride of life. Read the following passage of Scripture very slowly and yet loudly.

> For the desires of the flesh are opposed to the [Holy] Spirit, and the [desires of the] Spirit are opposed to the flesh (godless human nature); for these are antagonistic to each other [continually withstanding and in conflict with each other], so that you are not free *but* are prevented from doing what you desire to do. (Galatians 5:17)

The *you* here is the human spirit that is yielding to either the flesh or the Spirit of God. From this scripture we understand

Paul's battle, it was not that he willed, but being in bondage to the law through external duties in the flesh he cried for deliverance.

Now this should give us some reason to understand why there is so much opposition when one is led by God's Spirit to do and be in a certain type of ministry. Believers naturally weigh issues with the eyes of the flesh rather than their born-again spirit or *heart*, as the Bible calls it. Many church splits, murmurings, slanders, and false accusations would cease if believers learned to live a life led by the Spirit of God rather than their flesh (feelings). O what signs and wonders and display of God's glory we would see if only His people could walk led by the Spirit. There was abundance when Adam and Eve walked in the spirit.

Your flesh does not know control, subjection, or obedience to God, and the life of God is far from it. Let me tell you, if you are letting your mind of the flesh control you, you are not pleasing God, and God's acceptance is not about you but His love for you.

> So then those who are living the life of the flesh [catering to the appetites and impulses of their carnal nature] cannot please *or* satisfy God, *or* be acceptable to Him.

> But you are not living the life of the flesh, you are living the life of the Spirit, if the [Holy] Spirit of God [really] dwells within you [directs and controls you]. But if anyone does not possess the [Holy] Spirit of Christ, he is none of His [he does not belong to Christ, is not truly a child of God].

> But if Christ lives in you, [then although] your [natural] body is dead by reason of sin *and* guilt, the spirit is alive because of [the] righteousness [that He imputes to you].

> And if the Spirit of Him Who raised up Jesus from the dead dwells in you, [then] He Who raised up Christ *Jesus* from the dead will also restore to life your mortal (short-lived, perishable) bodies through His Spirit Who dwells in you.

> So then, brethren, we are debtors, but not to the flesh [we are not obligated to our carnal nature], to live [a life ruled by the standards set up by the dictates] of the flesh. (Romans 8:8–12)

I believe as you read these scriptures which the Lord told me to put there not to fill up pages but so that you will read them, your understanding of the purposes of God will grow.

The biggest and most successful lie the Devil has sold believers is that people are our enemies. No, they are not! You cannot expect to fight with people and have God hear your prayers.

Our enemies are not people. Not even our in-laws, not our brother or sister, husband or wife, not our neighbor or our employer or any human being. Nobody in their right mind would worship the Devil directly, and it would be easy to rebuke the Devil if we could see him openly, yet that is not the case. So we have what we know as doctrines of the Devil and the spirit of mammon. The Devil did not come directly to Adam; he came through an intermediary and got mistaken as just a little pet rather than a deadly enemy.

Believers have only one enemy: the Devil, Satan himself, and his evil spirits. Satan knows that if he can get you and keep you focused on seeing people as your enemy, then he can accomplish his plan against you and make you believe that God is doing it.

Now I just said he is our enemy, but that does not mean you go out there to win a fight against him. He is already defeated and that eternally. We fight to destroy all the arguments and knowledge that comes against the Word of the living God. Whether it is the experience of godly people or testimonies of someone's beliefs going away from the written Word of God, remember: *what is not supported by the Bible is not to be supported.*

> For though we walk (live) in the flesh, we are not carrying on our warfare according to the flesh *and* using mere human weapons.
>
> For the weapons of our warfare are not physical [weapons of flesh and blood], but they are mighty before God for the overthrow *and* destruction of strongholds ... (2 Corinthians 10:3–4),

What is this scripture telling us? Our fight is not with each other, no matter how it seems to our fleshly eyes. Stop fighting in the church, stop the backbiting, stop the slander, and stop the false accusations.

One thing the Lord showed me that has really helped in my life has been this word: *"Don't judge anyone from the outside till you have the power to tell what that person is thinking."*

Nobody knows what we are thinking, so how can we judge or preconceive a thought without any knowledge? You only know what somebody is thinking if they say it. *Don't assume things. You are not God, even though you may be right sometimes.*

> For we are not wrestling with flesh and blood [contending only with physical opponents], but against the despotisms, against the powers, against [the master spirits who are] the world rulers of this present darkness, against the spirit forces of wickedness in the heavenly (supernatural) sphere. (Ephesians 6:12)

Here again we see clearly emphasized that the battle is not against flesh and blood, that is to say human beings. Our fight is against the spirits of darkness and the knowledge of the world that goes against God's Word. When you are involved in a tight problem, don't ever conclude that the person you are having problems with is your enemy. The true enemy, Satan, uses human ignorance and lack of true perception to induce people to destroy each other. So instead of getting angry at a person, get angry with the Devil. Rebuke him out of the life of the person he has been deceiving, to use them against you, and see what miracles happen. Get into what the Word of God says in that situation, and solve the trouble.

CHAPTER 5

The Flesh

The lust of the eyes, the lust of the flesh, and pride of life, though three, can turn into one entity the Bible calls *the flesh* (the carnal nature, the old man.) Let me show you how it can hinder prayer and lead to unanswered prayer. Along the way, we will clarify how to realize the desired results to answered prayer.

> Without faith it is impossible to please *and* be satisfactory to Him. For whoever would come near to God must [necessarily] believe that God exists and that He is the rewarder of those who earnestly *and* diligently seek Him [out]. (Hebrews 11:6)

> So then those who are living the life of the flesh [catering to the appetites and impulses of their carnal nature] cannot please *or* satisfy God, *or* be acceptable to Him. (Romans 8:8)

Now this makes this very clear that you may claim all the faith it takes to receive mighty miracles. Still, God said that if you allow your flesh (carnal nature, unrenewed self) to live, then you are not pleasing toward God.

Some answers we receive from God because of His mercy, but pleasing Him is another issue altogether. God is pleased with us because of the sacrifice of Jesus, yet even that has to be received with an attitude of faith and not a temporary feeling.

The flesh is always in opposition to the walk of the spirit and vice versa. Living in the flesh is living with death along with all the miseries in life. God will not keep allowing blessings in a person's sinful state, working against the thought that people can continue in sin and be blessed.

> Now the mind of the flesh [which is sense and reason without the Holy Spirit] is death [death that comprises all the miseries arising from sin, both here and hereafter]. But the mind of the [Holy] Spirit is life and [soul] peace [both now and forever]. (Romans 8:6)

Living in the flesh is living in hostility with God and in rebellion against God.

> [That is] because the mind of the flesh [with its carnal thoughts and purposes] is hostile to God, for it does not submit itself to God's Law; indeed it cannot. (Romans 8:7)

Paul gives a very good example of a person when the flesh controls his life and keeps him from doing what is right before God:

> We know that the Law is spiritual; but I am a creature of the flesh [carnal, unspiritual], having been sold into slavery under [the control of] sin.

> For I do not understand my own actions [I am baffled, bewildered]. I do not practice *or* accomplish what I wish, but I do the very thing that I loathe [which my moral instinct condemns].

For I know that nothing good dwells within me, that is, in my flesh. I can will what is right, but I cannot perform it. [I have the intention and urge to do what is right, but no power to carry it out.]

For I fail to practice the good deeds I desire to do, but the evil deeds that I do not desire to do are what I am [ever] doing.

Now if I do what I do not desire to do, it is no longer I doing it [it is not myself that acts], but the sin [principle] which dwells within me [fixed and operating in my soul].

So I find it to be a law (rule of action of my being) that when I want to do what is right *and* good, evil is ever present with me *and* I am subject to its insistent demands. (Romans 7:14–15, 18–21)

How true it is that no good things dwell in our flesh. Don't waste time working to bring your flesh under control. That which is trying to live a holy life is the spirit of a born-again person. That flesh will never allow the spirit any breeding ground. The flesh creature must surely die before the new creature in Christ Jesus can live the will of God here on earth. Remember this, that the flesh gets its power from the law of God, basically the power of condemnation. *The life in the flesh is a life of condemnation and guilt.*

For I fail to practice the good deeds I desire to do, but the evil deeds that I do no desire to do are what I am (ever) doing.

Now if I do what I do not desire, I do it is no longer I doing it (it is not my self that acts) but the sin (principle) which dwells within me (fixing and operating in my soul.)

73

> So I find it to be a law (rule of action of my being)
> that when I want to do what is right *and* good
> evil is ever present with me *and* I am subject to
> insistent demands. (Romans 7:19–21)

Child of God, the Lord first reveals the nature of the problem
before He deals with it. Flesh exerts such upon the spirit, if not
put to death, that *all service done in the name of Jesus brings
glory to people, not to God, who is highly exalted forever.*

Any work that anyone does for God in the flesh is not at all
pleasing to God, no matter whether the world and the believers
circle decorates or honors the achievement. What really matters
is God's way. Jesus must always be the focal point and the center
of all we do and say and are.

> Except the Lord builds the house, they labor in
> vain who build it; except the Lord keeps the city,
> the watchman wakes but in vain. (Psalm 127:1)

> There is a way that seems right to a man *and*
> appears straight before him, but at the end of it is
> the way of death. (Proverbs 16:25)

(You could use *flesh* here for *man*, and this verse would mean
a whole lot more than before.) Let me show you something from
the Scriptures that shows the main goal and aim of the old man
(flesh).

> For the others all seek [to advance] their own
> interests, not those of Jesus Christ (the Messiah).
> (Philippians 2:21)

In the flesh, it's all about self and me. I really like the demonstration
that Joyce Meyer has on "What about Me! What about Me Me
Me!!!" The church of today lives in a very fleshly and touchy-feely

environment, and they resist any order, discipline, rebuking, or telling of wrong ways. To escape the hurt, before or after, they'll go to another church. To preach on holiness is similar to fighting the wind, no results at times.

The world lives in the church, and the Word is out where the world is to be.

What part does the world, with its system of operation, have to do with the flesh? More than you know. *With the flesh we touch the world of the seen sense.*

The world, with its ways of doing things, is where the flesh finds its comfort zone.

Let me show you what is God's mind on a world system controlled by Satan.

> Do not love *or* cherish the world or the things that are in the world. If anyone loves the world, love for the Father is not in him. (1 John 2:15)

You cannot love God and the world at the same time; if you believe that you can or that you do, you are a carnal believer, not matured in the Word of God. One great reason is because *all that the world produces is meant to feed the flesh (senses),* and in the flesh dwells nothing good and flesh does not please God.

> For he who sows to his own flesh (lower nature, sensuality) will from the flesh reap decay *and* ruin *and* destruction, but he who sows to the Spirit will from the Spirit reap eternal life. (Galatians 6:8)

If we feed the flesh—our senses and body—what it wants, the results are the ruin and entire destruction of all things good for us. What you feed will grow strong. If you feed your flesh with what it has always desired, it will always produce death and sin.

For the life of God is not found in the mind of the flesh but the spirit of a person. Living in strife, divisions, hate, and envy is all feeding to the flesh. This is what carnal believers do. There is no growth in carnal believers, who live by feeling and not by faith. For them, small issues matter more than spiritual things. The flesh rules supreme in a carnal believer, always seeking and never finding out. They are always getting their feelings hurt, and offence is their bread and butter.

> For you are still [unspiritual, having the nature] of the flesh [under the control of ordinary impulses]. For as long as [there are] envying and jealousy *and* wrangling and factions among you, are you not unspiritual *and* of the flesh, behaving yourselves after a human standard *and* like mere (unchanged) men? (1 Corinthians 3:3)

Let's go to the Scriptures and see the temptation that is presented to the flesh by means of the world.

> And the tempter came and said to Him, If You are God's Son, command these stones to be made [loaves of] bread.

> And he said to Him, If You are the Son of God, throw Yourself down; for it is written, He will give His angels charge over you, and they will bear you up on their hands, lest you strike your foot against a stone.

> Again, the Devil took Him up on a very high mountain and showed Him all the kingdoms of the

world and the glory (the splendor, magnificence, preeminence, and excellence) of them.

And he said to Him, These things, all taken together, I will give You, if You will prostrate Yourself before me and do homage *and* worship me. (Matthew 4:3, 6, 8–9)

If you notice carefully all temptation was based on worldly concerns that appealed to the flesh.

Satan finds access to your life through the weaknesses of one's flesh. I believe we are safe to say that being dead to the flesh means being alive to God. And being alive in the flesh is being dead to the Holy Spirit.

The devil's only access to your life is through your fleshly senses, and he uses thoughts to cause you to yield to temptations he provides by means of the world.

The sower sows the Word.

The ones along the path are those who have the Word sown [in their hearts], but when they hear, Satan comes at once and [by force] takes away the message which is sown in them.

And in the same way the ones sown upon stony ground are those who, when they hear the Word, at once receive *and* accept *and* welcome it with joy;

And they have no real root in themselves, and so they endure for a little while; then when trouble or persecution arises on account of the Word, they immediately are offended (become displeased, indignant, resentful) *and* they stumble *and* fall away.

> And the ones sown among the thorns are others who hear the Word;

> Then the cares *and* anxieties of the world *and* distractions of the age, and the pleasure *and* delight *and* false glamour *and* deceitfulness of riches, and the craving *and* passionate desire for other things creep in and choke *and* suffocate the Word, and it becomes fruitless. (Mark 4:14–19)

This explanation of the parable of the sower is about the way we understand and receive the Word of God in our life and how we apply it in our individual lives. *The Word of God is the source of life for the spirit of a born-again person.* Cut the source of power or support for a born-again spirit, and the flesh rules, and the spirit lies weak and dormant.

> And He humbled you and allowed you to hunger and fed you with manna, which you did not know nor did your fathers know, that He might make you recognize *and* personally know that man does not live by bread only, but man lives by every word that proceeds out of the mouth of the Lord. (Deuteronomy 8:3)

> He replied, It has been written, Man shall not live *and* be upheld *and* sustained by bread alone, but by every word that comes forth from the mouth of God. (Matthew 4:4)

Let me say again: the life of born-again people is kept and sustained by the *Word of God.* As manna fed the children of Israel, so the Word of God feeds the born-again child of God.

Now we know how needful it is for us to feed on the Word of God. Therefore, don't you think the enemy's major attack and temptation will also be based around this area, to steal the Word? Let's look at this parable once again.

> The ones along the path are those who have the Word sown [in their hearts], but when they hear, Satan comes at once and [by force] takes away the message which is sown in them. (Mark 4:15)

Why do persecution and trouble come? In order to steal the Word of God in you, lest it take root in you and make you strong. *Never allow yourself to be offended by the Word.* If the Word of God does not seem to go your way, don't get offended, but allow the Word right to show you what needs to be done in your life to get your provisions from God.

I have also learned that one way the Word takes no root is a lack of understanding of the Word. Learning is a process, and study has to take place for believers to know and understand what the Lord said. That way they will not be tossed to and fro with every wind of doctrine, since as I said the Devil will not come himself and steal the Word from you; rather, he will use your lack of understanding and faith in other things than the Word of God.

Then the cares *and* anxieties of the world *and* distractions of the age, and the pleasure *and* delight *and* false glamour *and* deceitfulness of riches, and the craving *and* passionate desire for other things creep in and choke *and* suffocate the Word, and it becomes fruitless. (Mark 4:19)

Now I believe it has become very clear in your mind that all attacks and temptations of the Devil are aimed at keeping the *Word of God* from being done in your life. Let's list some of the attacks presented in this verse:

❖ Cares
❖ Anxieties of the world

- ❖ Distractions of the age
- ❖ Pleasure
- ❖ Delight
- ❖ False glamour
- ❖ Deceitfulness of riches
- ❖ Cravings
- ❖ Passionate desire for other things than the Word of God

Now let's see this parable in action—a case study.

> On that same day [when] evening had come, He said to them, Let us go over to the other side [of the lake].
>
> And leaving the throng, they took Him with them, [just] as He was, in the boat [in which He was sitting]. And other boats were with Him.
>
> And a furious storm of wind [of hurricane proportions] arose, and the waves kept beating into the boat, so that it was already becoming filled.
>
> But He [Himself] was in the stern [of the boat], asleep on the [leather] cushion; and they awoke Him and said to Him, Master, do You not care that we are perishing?
>
> And He arose and rebuked the wind and said to the sea, Hush now! Be still (muzzled)! And the wind ceased (sank to rest as if exhausted by its beating) and there was [immediately] a great calm (a perfect peacefulness).
>
> He said to them, Why are you so timid *and* fearful? How is it that you have no faith (no firmly relying trust)?

> And they were filled with great awe *and* feared
> exceedingly and said one to another, Who then
> is this, that even wind and sea obey Him? (Mark
> 4:35–41)

It was on the same day that Jesus expounded on the parable of the sower and how the enemy comes in to steal the Word, that the disciples faced a storm. Yet Jesus had said to them, "Let us go to the other side"; note that if they sank, so would Jesus. But that would not have been the case, because Jesus was resting on the promise of Psalm 91.

Look at what the disciples said to him. "Don't you care that we perish?" *The cares of this world creep in to choke the Word.* I just listed for you things that the Devil uses to choke the Word out of your life, and one of them was *cares.* As Jews they knew the promises of God's protection from the Old Testament, and if they rested on them instead of worrying, they would still have made it to the other side.

Realize that sometimes you may know all there is to know about healing, protection, prosperity, peace, joy and love. Yet when the storms of life come in these areas, it becomes hard to practice them through times of trouble. The troubled situation speaks to you louder than the Word of God.

Fear had gripped the disciples, and they were far from the place of faith and trusting in the words of Jesus. We as believers need to develop a very strong faith in the person of Jesus and the words that He speaks, which He is able to perform. If you cannot trust and put your life on the line for the Word of God, you don't believe and trust Jesus. Jesus and His Word are one. Just going to church does not make one a believer; re-living Christ in your life does.

Don't allow demons, family members, friends, the storms of life, and temptations to steal the word God has given you through his

Word (Bible) and personally. Take God's Word, and speak to that storm of yours the Word that God has given you. You have power and authority over all the works of the enemy, and nothing shall by any means hurt you.

As you speak peace, peace will come, because everything in life and nature obeys the words of Jesus, for all things were created by Him, and all things are upheld by Him.

Understanding the world and its influence on the flesh is wonderfully expressed in the garden of Eden. The garden was God the Father's *kingdom rule* type. It's where His will was done and always should have been done. The Tree of Knowledge of Good and Evil is where the world is present, spreading her traps through outer beauty to attract the flesh to be aroused and fall into sin and disobedience of God almighty.

The Tree of Life represents Jesus, always ready to offer life eternal to whosoever will call upon His name and taste and see that He is good. The only tree the Lord instructed us not to eat from is the Tree of Knowledge of Good and Evil (the world system), for the day you eat of it you shall die. God did not stop Adam and Eve from touching and eating of the Tree of Life until they took hold of the world (the Tree of Knowledge of Good and Evil).

As long as you are walking with the Lord, you can partake of life. The moment you choose to touch the world—that is, your selfish, lustful methods of life—you are forbidden from partaking of life.

Flesh rules and has power over a person through enforcing its desires on the soul. With your spirit you touch God, who is spirit, and with your soul, you touch the world and its lusts. Your body only obeys what is in control. If the spirit is in control, it leads to the Word of God and His ways.

No spiritual revelation has been received in the flesh, which cannot receive it, nor does it understand it.

> Then Jesus answered him, Blessed (happy, fortunate, and to be envied) are you, Simon Bar-Jonah. For flesh and blood [men] have not revealed this to you, but My Father Who is in heaven. (Matthew 16:17)

> But the natural, nonspiritual man does not accept *or* welcome *or* admit into his heart the gifts *and* teachings *and* revelations of the Spirit of God, for they are folly (meaningless nonsense) to him; and he is incapable of knowing them [of progressively recognizing, understanding, and becoming better acquainted with them] because they are spiritually discerned *and* estimated *and* appreciated. (1 Corinthians 2:14)

Flesh does not and cannot receive the things of the spirit. Yet if you are spiritually minded as being led by the Holy Spirit and God's revealed Word, you can know His plans and purposes. Understanding the Bible is a spiritual matter.

Allow me to give you a few more verses on the flesh and then reveal to you from the Word of God steps you can take toward walking in the spirit and pleasing God, our heavenly Father. Let's look at Romans 8 a bit more.

> For those who are according to the flesh *and* are controlled by its unholy desires set their minds on *and* pursue those things which gratify the flesh, but those who are according to the Spirit *and* are controlled by the desires of the Spirit set their minds on *and* seek those things which gratify the [Holy] Spirit.

> Now the mind of the flesh [which is sense and reason without the Holy Spirit] is death [death that comprises all the miseries arising from sin, both here and hereafter]. But the mind of the [Holy] Spirit is life and [soul] peace [both now and forever].
>
> [That is] because the mind of the flesh [with its carnal thoughts and purposes] is hostile to God, for it does not submit itself to God's Law; indeed it cannot.
>
> So then those who are living the life of the flesh [catering to the appetites and impulses of their carnal nature] cannot please *or* satisfy God, *or* be acceptable to Him.
>
> But you are not living the life of the flesh, you are living the life of the Spirit, if the [Holy] Spirit of God [really] dwells within you [directs and controls you]. But if anyone does not possess the [Holy] Spirit of Christ, he is none of His [he does not belong to Christ, is not truly a child of God]. (Romans 8:5–9)

Let me point out some things for you. The flesh is not your bodily members; they are merely how the flesh gets power to express itself, the same way the Spirit of God inside you chooses to express Himself through your body parts.

The flesh is the set pattern of thinking, believing, and expressing things. It lives as a stronghold in one's mind. For the Bible lets us know that just as a person thinks, so that person. Flesh thoughts are fleshly and spirit thoughts spiritual.

Romans 8 expresses this point clearly, saying that to be carnally minded (fleshly minded) is death. The flesh tends to exalt itself above everyone and everything. Therefore Paul lets us know:

> [We] refute arguments *and* theories *and* reasonings and every proud *and* lofty thing that sets itself up against the [true] knowledge of God; and we lead every thought *and* purpose away captive into the obedience of Christ (the Messiah, the Anointed One) ... (2 Corinthians 10:5)

Look at those words closely. In the King James Version, we read: "Casting down imaginations, and every high thing that exalteth itself ... and ... every thought." These are expressed by the bodily members yet live in your mind (thought, will, emotion). When Adam and Eve were tempted, that was what they should have done to the thoughts arising in the flesh: casting them down and showing the Devil the door off Planet Earth. The flesh is the natural person, including the unrenewed will and mind, moving in the world of self and sense only. Everything we have learned in our fallen state needs to be unlearned, and new lessons of life from God's Word must be implanted in the garden of our heart and mind.

Self-imposed ordinances gratify the flesh. The self (flesh) has no desire or place for obedience to anyone except to please itself. Self is empowered by the untrained mind (the natural person).

Self and untrained mind are not subject to God and are always in opposition to God's Spirit in a person. Sin is expressed in the bodily members empowered by the untrained mind, where the temptation to sin was birthed and acted upon long before it was enacted by your bodily members.

That is the reason God emphasizes on renewing our mind by the Word of God to think, act, and speak according to God's plan, laid down in the Bible for our benefit.

The law was enacted to be obeyed through outward duties performed by your bodily members and had not much bearing on people's inner spirit. Yet we know the flesh cannot and will not subject itself to someone else's rule over it; so the flesh rebels and pays the price of sin. *Sin finds itself strengthened by its access to the bodily members.*

It is something to know that every person's opinion is right in their own eyes, and no one wants to be found wrong. Once I said to a brother in the Lord, "We have only images and beliefs that we have learned; what we don't know causes us trouble. We don't want to change, to learn things better, and bring the changes necessary. Many refuse, since it seems hard, and yes, it is hard to die to your being wrong. Death and the willingness to let go produce the life that is worth the living in Christ."

Jesus came in the flesh, fulfilled the law of God in the flesh, died in the flesh, and overcame it totally. His sacrificial death on the cross was enough to put sin and flesh forever out of our lives and let us follow and obey the law of God, empowered by the help of the Holy Spirit and our faith in the complete work of Jesus on Calvary. Praise God.

CHAPTER 6

Putting the Flesh to Death

As a believer you do not tame the flesh, control the flesh, or suppress the flesh. *You need to put the flesh to death with its desires and beliefs.* Death of the flesh is the only way to live led by the Spirit of God.

Let's take a trip through the different places where the Bible talks about dying to the flesh.

> I have been crucified with Christ [in Him I have shared His crucifixion]; it is no longer I who live, but Christ (the Messiah) lives in me; and the life I now live in the body I live by faith in (by adherence to and reliance on and complete trust in) the Son of God, Who loved me and gave Himself up for me. (Galatians 2:20)

> But I say, walk *and* live [habitually] in the [Holy] Spirit [responsive to *and* controlled *and* guided by the Spirit]; then you will certainly not gratify the cravings *and* desires of the flesh (of human nature without God).

> And those who belong to Christ Jesus (the Messiah) have crucified the flesh (the godless

human nature) with its passions and appetites *and* desires.

If we live by the [Holy] Spirit, let us also walk by the Spirit. [If by the Holy Spirit we have our life in God, let us go forward walking in line, our conduct controlled by the Spirit.] (Galatians 5:16, 24–25)

Our dying is not one of physical suffering to learn lessons so we may live better. We live out the inward spiritual reality in our intellect and soul, lining up with the purpose and thoughts of God. We go on declaring what God has said about us, and by meditation on that Word, we make those spiritual realities manifest in our soul and physical life.

I believe that the Lord desires for me to give you more scriptures to read for yourself. Let the Holy Spirit speak to your heart as you go through them, slowly and thoughtfully, repeatedly if need be. Some spiritual realities can be thought through, yet in Christ we must go through many experiences for ourselves to grasp them. Once we can find ourselves in the Word of God, all that's left is to do what the Word says about us.

Jesus was talked about as coming in the volume of the book (see Psalm 40:7; Hebrews 10:7), and He lived out His entire life in the fulfilment of the prophecies about Him. As you go through these scriptures, *find yourself in them, and LIVE IT OUT.*

What shall we say [to all this]? Are we to remain in sin in order that God's grace (favor and mercy) may multiply *and* overflow?

Certainly not! How can we who died to sin live in it any longer?

Are you ignorant of the fact that all of us who have been baptized into Christ Jesus were baptized into His death?

We were buried therefore with Him by the baptism into death, so that just as Christ was raised from the dead by the glorious [power] of the Father, so we too might [habitually] live *and* behave in newness of life.

For if we have become one with Him by sharing a death like His, we shall also be [one with Him in sharing] His resurrection [by a new life lived for God].

We know that our old (unrenewed) self was nailed to the cross with Him in order that [our] body [which is the instrument] of sin might be made ineffective *and* inactive for evil, that we might no longer be the slaves of sin.

For when a man dies, he is freed (loosed, delivered) from [the power of] sin [among men].

Now if we have died with Christ, we believe that we shall also live with Him,

Because we know that Christ (the Anointed One), being once raised from the dead, will never die again; death no longer has power over Him.

For by the death He died, He died to sin [ending His relation to it] once for all; and the life that He lives, He is living to God [in unbroken fellowship with Him].

Even so consider yourselves also dead to sin *and* your relation to it broken, but alive to God [living in unbroken fellowship with Him] in Christ Jesus.

Let not sin therefore rule as king in your mortal (short-lived, perishable) bodies, to make you yield to its cravings *and* be subject to its lusts *and* evil passions.

Do not continue offering or yielding your bodily members [and faculties] to sin as instruments (tools) of wickedness. But offer *and* yield yourselves to God as though you have been raised from the dead to [perpetual] life, and your bodily members [and faculties] to God, presenting them as implements of righteousness.

For sin shall not [any longer] exert dominion over you, since now you are not under Law [as slaves], but under grace [as subjects of God's favor and mercy].

What then [are we to conclude]? Shall we sin because we live not under Law but under God's favor *and* mercy? Certainly not!

Do you not know that if you continually surrender yourselves to anyone to do his will, you are the slaves of him whom you obey, whether that be to sin, which leads to death, or to obedience which leads to righteousness (right doing and right standing with God)?

But thank God, though you were once slaves of sin, you have become obedient with all your heart to the standard of teaching in which you were instructed *and* to which you were committed.

And having been set free from sin, you have become the servants of righteousness (of conformity to the divine will in thought, purpose, and action).

I am speaking in familiar human terms because of your natural limitations. For as you yielded your bodily members [and faculties] as servants to impurity and ever increasing lawlessness, so now yield your bodily members [and faculties] once for all as servants

to righteousness (right being and doing) [which leads] to sanctification.

For when you were slaves of sin, you were free in regard to righteousness.

But then what benefit (return) did you get from the things of which you are now ashamed? [None] for the end of those things is death.

But now since you have been set free from sin and have become the slaves of God, you have your present reward in holiness and its end is eternal life.

For the wages which sin pays is death, but the [bountiful] free gift of God is eternal life through (in union with) Jesus Christ our Lord. (Romans 6:1–23)

I have often heard people say that we appropriate the death to the flesh by faith and confession. And yes, that is true partially. However, not only do we need to appropriate by faith our being dead to sin by the sacrifice of Jesus; we also need to put to death daily the so-called flesh and its carnal desires. We do that every time we yield to the Word and Spirit of God instead of yielding to temptations that are presented to us.

Let's see what our Lord Jesus taught His disciples about being His disciple.

> And He said to all, If any person wills to come after Me, let him deny himself [disown himself, forget, lose sight of himself and his own interests, refuse and give up himself] and take up his cross daily and follow Me [cleave steadfastly to Me, conform wholly to My example in living and, if need be, in dying also]. (Luke 9:23)

What a price for discipleship, yet every word is worth the doing. Do you realize the term *HIS CROSS DAILY*? I believe this is what our everyday prayer of consecration ought to be: *"Lord, I choose to follow You wholly today, I choose again to carry the cross of death to self, so You can live through my life completely. Not my way or my will, but Thy will be done in me. Amen."* When you die to self and allow the Lord to take over, *grace flows unhindered.*

One disciple of Jesus understood this principle well. Not only did he have the revelation of our being dead in Christ to sin (that separates us from God and heaven). He also knew that there is flesh that needs to be put to death daily in order that the Lord Jesus' will in our lives may prosper. That man was the apostle Paul:

> [I assure you] by the pride which I have in you in [your fellowship and union with] Christ Jesus our Lord, that I die daily [I face death every day and die to self]. (1 Corinthians 15:31)

Not only was Paul facing literal death threats from situations and people around him, he was also daily putting in near death experiences so his soul and intellect might not be exalted through the abundance of revelation being given to him. Paul's "thorn in the flesh," a messenger of Satan continually standing against him, was actually working to his advantage from keeping him from being lifted up in pride. *See where the thorn was causing trouble, the flesh. For all sin of self is found in the flesh. You find grace when you stop striving.*

This same Paul in **1 Corinthians 9:26–27** says:

> Therefore I do not run uncertainly (without definite aim). I do not box like one beating the air *and* striking without an adversary.

> But [like a boxer] I buffet my body [handle it roughly, discipline it by hardships] and subdue it, for fear that after proclaiming to others the Gospel *and* things pertaining to it, I myself should become unfit [not stand the test, be unapproved and rejected as a counterfeit].

Paul says, "I discipline my body," showing that there has been a change in who's in command of Paul's body. His born-again spirit disciplines his body (flesh) to bring it daily into subjection to the spirit man. The ways of God to him were more important than personal gratifications.

Let me show you what could have been in Paul's mind when speaking and writing about death:

> So kill (deaden, deprive of power) the evil desire lurking in your members [those animal impulses and all that is earthly in you that is employed in sin]: sexual vice, impurity, sensual appetites,

unholy desires, and all greed *and* covetousness, for that is idolatry (the deifying of self and other created things instead of God).

And [clothe] yourselves with the new [spiritual self], which is [ever in the process of being] renewed *and* remolded into [fuller and more perfect knowledge upon] knowledge after the image (the likeness) of Him Who created it. (Colossians 3:5, 10)

Please, if you want to see a revelation of crucifixion of self and the flesh, read the above passage of Scripture again. If need be, read it again till it sinks down deep in your mind and spirit. You will need to tell your animal impulses that they have no right in your born-again self. Deprive of power the desires and impurity that rise against God and the Word of God. I really like the word *kill*: make it lie in complete uselessness, as a dead member of your body.

For it is written that Abraham had two sons, one by the bondmaid and one by the free woman.

But whereas the child of the slave woman was born according to the flesh *and* had an ordinary birth, the son of the free woman was born in fulfillment of the promise.

But what does the Scripture say? Cast out *and* send away the slave woman and her son, for never shall the son of the slave woman be heir *and* share the inheritance with the son of the free woman.

So, brethren, we [who are born again] are not children of a slave woman [the natural], but of the free [the supernatural]. (Galatians 4: 22–23, 30–31)

I believe by now the Spirit of the living God is causing you to see that the flesh must be completely put to death and out of sight. Let me share with you a few points that will help you understand the above scriptures better:

The slave woman's child was a part of the same household, as the flesh is part of our body.

The slave woman's child could not inherit possessions in the house, as our flesh will neither please God nor receive any of the inheritance promised to the spirit-ruled man.

The child of the flesh always despised and persecuted the child of the spirit. In the same way, so long as the flesh is alive in us, it despises and does its best to suppress the spirit's full control and leadership in our lives.

Casting out the slave woman with her child did not mean they were dead, yet in Abraham's mind they were dead to him. So it is with our flesh: though we know the flesh is there with us, to put it to death is to consider it as good as dead and its rule and power over our born-again spirit destroyed. The spirit of the born-again believer now rules over the whole body in line with the Word of God. The spirit now despises and puts down the flesh, even if it tries to come back. *It's too late, flesh; the spirit rules.* Once the promised child has grown up, nobody comes in and overthrows him. He is fully developed and mature in his own right, and he can take his stand based on his right as a son.

The unrenewed and untrained natural man, the flesh with all its ideals and thoughts, must be challenged with the Word of God. Just as a caterpillar changes the outer physical makeup, inwardly he remains a caterpillar but with a completely new outlook. The change that God made happened inside us, and it must be seen outside. Baptism works on the same principle: we outwardly proclaim the inward change.

And if your hand puts a stumbling block before you *and* causes you to sin, cut it off! It is more profitable *and* wholesome for you to go into life [that is really worthwhile] maimed than with two hands to go to hell (Gehenna), into the fire that cannot be put out.

And if your foot is a cause of stumbling *and* sin to you, cut it off! It is more profitable *and* wholesome for you to enter into life [that is really worthwhile] crippled than, having two feet, to be cast into hell (Gehenna).

And if your eye causes you to stumble *and* sin, pluck it out! It is more profitable *and* wholesome for you to enter the kingdom of God with one eye than with two eyes to be thrown into hell (Gehenna). (Mark 9:43, 45, 47)

I repeat that the Devil's arena of attack is the fleshly mind. Here the Lord Jesus makes it easy to understand that if any member of our body causes us to sin or disobey God's Word, we are better off without it. From there it is no great leap to realize that pleasing God enables believers to enter into all that God has in store for them. I believe that these scriptures very clearly show us what God wants done with the flesh and its animal desires: they are to be put to death. Every time a voice of the fleshly mind calls, you call upon the Word of God and be saved from your trouble.

The apostle Paul's revelation of living in the spirit:

Therefore we do not become discouraged (utterly spiritless, exhausted, and wearied out through fear). Though our outer man is [progressively] decaying *and* wasting away, yet our inner self is being [progressively] renewed day after day. (2 Corinthians 4:16)

The flesh is dying naturally and losing strength day by day as time goes by; that's our natural human body. Yet our inner spirit never grows old. Things in the flesh are judged into death, but on the spiritual path we are ever being renewed and grow stronger as we abide in the vine continually.

I have read something that I believe will be a blessing to you from the classic devotion: *My Utmost for His Highest* by Oswald Chambers.

The Relinquished Life
"I am crucified with Christ." (Galatians 2:20)

No one is ever united with Jesus Christ until he is willing to relinquish not sin only, but his whole way of looking at things. To be born from above by the Spirit of God means that we must let go before we lay hold and in the first stages it is the relinquishing of all pretence. What our Lord wants us to present to him is not goodness, nor honesty nor endeavor, but real solid sin that is all he can take from us. And what does he give in exchange for our sins? *Real solid righteousness.* But we must relinquish all pretence of being anything all claims of being worthy of God's consideration. Then the Spirit of God will show us what further there is relinquish. There has to be relinquishing of my claim to my right to myself in every phase. Am I willing to relinquish my hold on all possess, my hold on my affections and on everything and be identified with the death of Christ Jesus. There is always a sharp, painful disillusion to go through before we do relinquish. When a man really sees himself as the Lord sees him, it is not abominable sins of the flesh that shock him, but the awful nature of the pride of his own heart against Jesus Christ. When he sees himself in the light of the Lord, the shame and the horror and the desperate conviction come home.

If you are up against the question of relinquishing go through the crisis, relinquish all, and God will make you fit for all that he requires of you.

Moral Decision about Sin
"Knowing this, that out old man is crucified with him, that the body of sin might be destroyed, that henceforth we should not serve sin." (Romans 6:6)

Lo crucifixion. Have I made this decision about sin, that it must be killed right out in me? It takes a long time to come to a moral decision about sin, but it is the greatest moment in my life when I do decide that just as Jesus Christ died for the sin of the world, so sin must die out on me, not be curbed or suppressed or counteracted, but crucified. No one can bring anyone else to this decision. We may be earnestly convinced and religiously convinced, but what we need to do is to come to the decision which Paul forces here.

Haul yourself up take a time alone with God, make the moral decision and say, "Lord identify me with the death until I know that sin is dead in me". To make the moral decision that sin in you must be put to death.

It was not a divine anticipation on the part of Paul, but a very radical and definite experience am I prepared to let the Spirit of God search me until I know what the disposition of sin is the thing that lusts against the spirit of God in me? Then, if so, will I agree with God's verdict on the disposition of sin- that it should be identified with the death of Jesus? I cannot reckon myself "dead indeed unto sin" unless I have been through this radical issue of the will before God. Have I entered into the glorious privileges of being crucified with Christ until all that is left is the life of Christ in my flesh and blood? "I am crucified with Christ, nevertheless I live, but Christ lives in me".

The Realm of the Real
"In your patience possess ye your souls." (Luke 21:19)

When a man is born again, there is not the same robustness in his thinking or reasoning for a time as formerly. We have to make an expression of the new life to form the mind of Christ. "Acquire your soul with patience". Many of us prefer to stay at the threshold of the Believer's life instead of going on to construct a soul in accordance with the new life God has put within. We fail because we are ignorant of the way we are made. We put things down to the Devil instead of our own undisciplined nature. Think what we can be when we are aroused. There are certain things that we must not pray about, moods for instances. Moods never go by praying, moods go by kicking. A mood nearly always has its seat in the physical condition, not in the moral. It is a continual effect not to listen to the moods which arise from a physical condition, never submit to them for a second. We have to take ourselves by the scruff of the neck and shake ourselves and we will find that we can do what we said we could not. The case with most of us is that we won't. The Believer's life is one of incarnate spiritual pluck.

Let me briefly expose the flesh, we put to death. We must learn to first identify our adversary before we overcome it.

I once more protest *and* testify to every man who receives circumcision that he is under obligation *and* bound to practice the whole of the Law *and* its ordinances.

If you seek to be justified *and* declared righteous *and* to be given a right standing with God through the Law, you are brought to nothing *and* so separated (severed) from Christ. You have fallen away from grace (from God's gracious favor and unmerited blessing).

For we, [not relying on the Law but] through the [Holy] Spirit's [help], by faith anticipate *and* wait for the blessing *and* good for which our righteousness *and* right standing with God [our conformity to His will in purpose, thought, and action, causes us] to hope.

For [if we are] in Christ Jesus, neither circumcision nor uncircumcision counts for anything, but only faith activated *and* energized *and* expressed *and* working through love.

You were running the race nobly. Who has interfered in (hindered and stopped you from) your heeding *and* following the Truth?

This [evil] persuasion is not from Him Who called you [Who invited you to freedom in Christ].

A little leaven (a slight inclination to error, or a few false teachers) leavens the whole lump [it perverts the whole conception of faith or misleads the whole church].

[For my part] I have confidence [toward you] in the Lord that you will take no contrary view of the matter *but* will come to think with me. But he who is unsettling you, whoever he is, will have to bear the penalty.

But, brethren, if I still preach circumcision [as some accuse me of doing, as necessary to salvation], why am I still suffering persecution? In that case the cross has ceased to be a stumbling block *and* is made meaningless (done away).

I wish those who unsettle *and* confuse you would [go all the way and] cut themselves off!

For you, brethren, were [indeed] called to freedom; only [do not let your] freedom be an incentive to your flesh *and* an opportunity *or* excuse [for selfishness], but through love you should serve one another.

For the whole Law [concerning human relationships] is complied with in the one precept, You shall love your neighbor as [you do] yourself.

But if you bite and devour one another [in partisan strife], be careful that you [and your whole fellowship] are not consumed by one another.

But I say, walk *and* live [habitually] in the [Holy] Spirit [responsive to *and* controlled *and* guided by the Spirit]; then you will certainly not gratify the cravings *and* desires of the flesh (of human nature without God).

For the desires of the flesh are opposed to the [Holy] Spirit, and the [desires of the] Spirit are opposed to the flesh (godless human nature); for these are antagonistic to each other [continually withstanding and in conflict with each other], so that you are not free *but* are prevented from doing what you desire to do.

But if you are guided (led) by the [Holy] Spirit, you are not subject to the Law.

Now the doings (practices) of the flesh are clear (obvious): they are immorality, impurity, indecency,

Idolatry, sorcery, enmity, strife, jealousy, anger (ill temper), selfishness, divisions (dissensions), party spirit (factions, sects with peculiar opinions, heresies),

Envy, drunkenness, carousing, and the like. I warn you beforehand, just as I did previously, that those who do such things shall not inherit the kingdom of God. (Galatians 5:3–21)

But immorality (sexual vice) and all impurity [of lustful, rich, wasteful living] or greediness must not even be named among you, as is fitting *and* proper among saints (God's consecrated people).

Let there be no filthiness (obscenity, indecency) nor foolish *and* sinful (silly and corrupt) talk, nor coarse jesting, which are not fitting *or* becoming; but instead voice your thankfulness [to God].

For be sure of this: that no person practicing sexual vice or impurity in thought or in life, or one who is covetous [who has lustful desire for the property of others and is greedy for gain]—for he [in effect] is an idolater--has any inheritance in the kingdom of Christ and of God.

Let no one delude *and* deceive you with empty excuses *and* groundless arguments [for these sins], for through these things the wrath of God comes upon the sons of rebellion *and* disobedience.

So do not associate *or* be sharers with them.

For once you were darkness, but now you are light in the Lord; walk as children of Light [lead the lives of those native-born to the Light].

For the fruit (the effect, the product) of the Light *or the Spirit* [consists] in every form of kindly goodness, uprightness of heart, and trueness of life.

And try to learn [in your experience] what is pleasing to the Lord [let your lives be constant proofs of what is most acceptable to Him].

Take no part in *and* have no fellowship with the fruitless deeds *and* enterprises of darkness, but instead [let your lives be so in contrast as to] expose *and* reprove *and* convict them.

For it is a shame even to speak of *or* mention the things that [such people] practice in secret.

But when anything is exposed *and* reproved by the light, it is made visible *and* clear; and where everything is visible *and* clear there is light.

Therefore He says, Awake, O sleeper, and arise from the dead, and Christ shall shine (make day dawn) upon you *and* give you light.

Look carefully then how you walk! Live purposefully *and* worthily *and* accurately, not as the unwise *and* witless, but as wise (sensible, intelligent people),

Making the very most of the time [buying up each opportunity], because the days are evil.

Therefore do not be vague *and* thoughtless *and* foolish, but understanding *and* firmly grasping what the will of the Lord is.

And do not get drunk with wine, for that is debauchery; but ever be filled *and* stimulated with the [Holy] Spirit. (Ephesians 5:3–18)

When the Spirit is at work in you, the flesh is dead on account of the Lordship of the Spirit's control. Can you picture the mastery our Lord Jesus had over the flesh, that despite knowing the pain He had to physically bear on His body, He chose to do the will of God over His bodily sufferings? He'd rather suffer in His flesh than disobey the Spirit's call for His life.

Are we willing to suffer in the flesh rather than disobey the Master's call in our life? To always remember that disobedience is sin and brings the curse, yet *obedience brings a blessing*?

Yet there are incidents when believers of Jesus suffer for the foolish decisions and actions they take in life and then blame it on God or the devil.

> [And see to it that] your conscience is entirely clear (unimpaired), so that, when you are falsely accused as evildoers, those who threaten you abusively *and* revile your right behavior in Christ may come to be ashamed [of slandering your good lives].
>
> For [it is] better to suffer [unjustly] for doing right, if that should be God's will, than to suffer [justly] for doing wrong.
>
> For Christ [the Messiah Himself] died for sins once for all, the Righteous for the unrighteous (the Just for the unjust, the Innocent for the guilty), that He might bring us to God. In His human body He was put to death, but He was made alive in the spirit ... (1 Peter 3:16–18)

Don't think you are suffering for Jesus being spoken badly of, when you really are acting badly. Your suffering must be justified.

Now look at the words in verse 18: He was put to death but made alive in the spirit. Now that is what it is all about: *alive in the spirit and dead to the flesh.*

Just have a look at the teaching of Jesus concerning the vine and branches. The beauty of a crucified life is the outcome that it brings *abundant fruit*. Pruning is a continual work that takes place in the life of the branch so that the branch may be fruitful. Read the following:

> I am the True Vine, and My Father is the Vinedresser.
>
> Any branch in Me that does not bear fruit [that stops bearing] He cuts away (trims off, takes away); and He cleanses *and* repeatedly prunes every branch that continues to bear fruit, to make it bear more *and* richer *and* more excellent fruit.
>
> You are cleansed *and* pruned already, because of the word which I have given you [the teachings I have discussed with you].
>
> Dwell in Me, and I will dwell in you. [Live in Me, and I will live in you.] Just as no branch can bear fruit of itself without abiding in (being vitally united to) the vine, neither can you bear fruit unless you abide in Me.
>
> I am the Vine; you are the branches. Whoever lives in Me and I in him bears much (abundant) fruit. However, apart from Me [cut off from vital union with Me] you can do nothing. (John 15:1–5)

Take a look again at verse two: "He cleanses and repeatedly prunes every branch that continues to bear fruit, to make it bear more and richer and more excellent fruit." Even if you are bearing fruit, you need pruning at some point, so you may bear yet more fruit. God reveals the dark areas not to condemn you but to make you strong in those areas, a vessel worthy of the master's use.

Another great picture of a crucified life includes letting go of things that may not be wrong but hinder your progress and growth in the Lord.

> Therefore then, since we are surrounded by so great a cloud of witnesses [who have borne testimony to the Truth], let us strip off *and* throw aside every encumbrance (unnecessary weight) and that sin which so readily (deftly and cleverly) clings to *and* entangles us, and let us run with patient endurance *and* steady *and* active persistence the appointed course of the race that is set before us ... (Hebrews 12:1)

The writer here by the Holy Spirit is telling us to strip off and throw aside. You don't put on what you throw away; you put the new where the old used to be. You strip off the old paint and put new on; you throw away old clothes and put on new, freshly washed garments. There is no recycling but rather a completely new product. *Whatever mind-set you will not die to or renew will be the very thing that will hold you in bondage.*

> Put on God's whole armor [the armor of a heavy-armed soldier which God supplies], that you may be able successfully to stand up against [all] the strategies *and* the deceits of the Devil. (Ephesians 6:11)

Temptation's main aim—to cause us to sin by disobeying the Word of God—shows here an interesting characteristic: it is defiant and clever. The temptation is defiant at times and has a stubborn nature. The very fact that you have resisted and confessed God's Word induces it to stick around and keep trying to work its way back. You have to stand on the Word and promises of God and keep standing. You continue to deny the temptation right in your life and family. *What you continue to stand against, you will overcome. What you continue to fight will leave your life for good.*

See in the following examples how sin continues to defy the righteous.

> And He rescued righteous Lot, greatly worn out *and* distressed by the wanton ways of the ungodly *and* lawless—
>
> For that just man, living [there] among them, tortured his righteous soul every day with what he saw and heard of [their] unlawful and wicked deeds … (2 Peter 2:7–8)
>
> The Lord saw that the wickedness of man was great in the earth, and that every imagination *and* intention of all human thinking was only evil continually.
>
> And the Lord regretted that He had made man on the earth, and He was grieved at heart.
>
> So the Lord said, I will destroy, blot out, *and* wipe away mankind, whom I have created from the face of the ground—not only man, [but] the beasts and the creeping things and the birds of the air—for it grieves Me *and* makes Me regretful that I have made them.
>
> But Noah found grace (favor) in the eyes of the Lord. (Genesis 6:5–8)

There is a death that brings life, which most believers are not aware of. There is a powerful weapon called *absolute surrender* of my will and self in the hands of our Maker. We as believers will never know the true meaning of living a believer's life till we leave, like our Master Jesus, who from His birth was *born to be crucified.*

> I assure you, most solemnly I tell you, Unless a grain of wheat falls into the earth and dies, it remains [just one grain; it never becomes more but lives] by itself alone. But if it dies, it produces many others *and* yields a rich harvest.
>
> Anyone who loves his life loses it, but anyone who hates his life in this world will keep it to life eternal. [Whoever has no love for, no concern for, no regard for his life here on earth, but despises it, preserves his life forever and ever.]
>
> If anyone serves Me, he must continue to follow Me [to cleave steadfastly to Me, conform wholly to My example in living and, if need be, in dying] and wherever I am, there will My servant be also. If anyone serves Me, the Father will honor him. (John 12:24–26)

Flesh, as I said earlier, cannot be tamed, it must be crucified and put to death, then and only then can the life of God inside us show forth the full glory and beauty of our new birth. Jesus laid down the principle for His disciples to follow, that death in itself is not a thing to be feared but a process starter to a new life we never can experience till we die. The same is true in natural death: we pass from the physical to the spiritual, and based on our choice whether to believe on the cross and sacrifice of Jesus, we go either to heaven or hell. Yet the process was started through death.

What a wonderful life in Christ is waiting for believers who choose to die to self and live the rest of their earthly life as bondservants of the Lord Jesus. If you ever do a study of the word *to serve* in the Bible, you will see that the only reason God brought out the children of Israel from bondage was so they would serve Him in love. Paul uses the same word for himself as bondslave of Christ, identifying himself as a bondservant of Jesus.

To serve was to die to one's right of being commander, living instead under the command and rule of another. One word to describe service is to *worship*, and once we use the word *service* in worship, it will mean a great lot more than we know. Jesus said the Father seeks those who will worship Him. If we substitute for the word, we can see that the Father seeks those who will serve Him.

Worship in modern terms is where we make a choice, but in serving, He makes the choice, and we follow.

The reason temptation can forcibly drive people to fall into its trap is that believers have not yet come to the complete realization of the Bible truth of the One to whom their spirit, soul, and body belong. Jesus paid a very high price to buy us back, yet He will not force his Lordship over our lives in this dispensation of grace. However, a time is coming when He will rule from Jerusalem, and then shall all the people of the earth worship Him.

The church must know and come to know this well: we are not our own, and to be a believer is to live, do, speak, go, get up, and sit down at the direction and will of the Master, Jesus.

That is what the Devil desires from the beginning, and so he has to use fear to make people serve him. Our God is not like that; He gives you and me a choice to surrender.

Did you know that all the apostles died and were martyred except John the beloved, who died a natural death? Each one paid a price for their faith and for the sake of the gospel they did not count their life of much value in order that we might hear and know the good news of salvation.

What price are we really willing to pay for the power of God in our lives and ministries? What will you do when the rubber meets the road and there is pain and accusation against you for the sake of the message you preach? Will you change it to please people, or rather will you preach ever more strongly? The reward is for the overcomer.

CHAPTER 7

Holy Unto the Lord

> Now if [all these things are true, then be sure] the Lord
> knows how to rescue the godly out of temptations *and*
> trials, and how to keep the ungodly under chastisement
> until the Day of Judgment *and* doom ... (2 Peter 2:9)

This is indeed a glorious truth that gives us strength and assurance that we shall overcome and be victorious over all temptations that come our way. Every temptation is to be overcome. Though you may be strong, yet it's not your strength that gives victory, but the faithfulness of God that will see you through.

Yet, child of God, you must learn to avoid all possible occasions of temptation. Wise people keep themselves as far as they can from the edge. This would mean there are some things you had better never touch, books you'd better never read, pictures you'd better never see, some people you'd better never know, certain websites you'd better never visit, and places you'd better keep away from.

Let me share with you some wonderful truths I learned from J. Oswald Sanders' book on *Men from God's School*. His thoughts about Joseph and Samson I believe will really bless you.

First, concerning the life of Joseph, he writes that sex attraction is perhaps the strongest lure of mankind. It is both a test and temptation. It makes or breaks a man. On Joseph's temptation by Potiphar's wife, I gathered some great points from his book: *"The temptation gathered strength from the fact that it was totally unexpected. It came at an unexpected time."*

The Devil waits for his opportunity to put you down to sin and bring you the consequences of sin. When your mind is put in a situation where it is given an opportunity to fall, most likely it will. So he waits till everything is going well at home, church, and work, and when you least expect it, he throws one. That is why a believer is called a soldier, to be alert and ready to put away every attack of the enemy and the carnal mind. Jesus therefore told His disciples to *watch* (stay wide awake) and pray that you enter not into temptation.

"The temptation was more irresistible because of its Daily Repetition." Day after day, Potiphar's wife enticed Joseph to sleep with her, yet day after day Joseph resisted her offer. Child of God, the Devil is persistent at throwing temptation your way so as to weaken your resistance. Your desire for living a holy life must go beyond to the point of such resistance that the enemy's persistence to induce you to yield only serves to toughen your resolve.

"Another element in the fierceness of the temptation was that of Favorable Opportunity. The Devil selects the most auspicious occasion to bungle his fiery darts."

There was no one found in the home and what better moment to throw these temptations than now. Keep yourselves from every appearance of evil.

> Desire is not wrong, and temptation is not sin—otherwise our much tempted Lord would have been a sinful man. *The temptation becomes sin only when we gratify legitimate desire from*

> *illegitimate sources or to an excessive degree. To voluntarily walk into the zone of temptation is to forfeit our claim to divine help.* There may be times when the flames of passion are so hot that the only escape is a clean pair of heels and the king's highway. To linger and dally with temptation is to fall for in a battle between imagination and the will, it is always the imagination that wins. Kill the serpent; don't stroke it.

After Joseph had been promoted to Prime Minister of Egypt, there was another temptation, only in a different form. This time it was wealth. *"It is common to be less disciplined in prosperity than in adversity."* Let me take your attention to a very wonderful place in the New Testament that reveals this truth further.

> But those who crave to be rich fall into temptation and a snare and into many foolish (useless, godless) and hurtful desires that plunge men into ruin *and* destruction and miserable perishing. (1 Timothy 6:9)

Money is not sin till you start to crave for it more than for God Himself. For it is God who gives us the ability to become rich. If we go after riches without God, we shall fall into a multitude of temptations, and the result will be ruin and destruction.

You can be sure that the Devil will never come as he is and stand and tell a person, "I am going to tempt you now. Let us see if you can stand this." As far-fetched as this seems, he does not come this way. Rather, he deceives and lies, making man choose between God and mammon. He never compares or brings his name in comparison with God, since it's his immediate loss. Even when he tested the Master, he said, "All this wealth will I give Thee"; it's always something to gratify the flesh.

Jesus also said that man cannot serve or worship God and mammon, no devil mentioned here. Yet when Adam fell, God saw that hearing the enemy's words above His was transgression. Consider the life of David as J. Oswald Sanders goes ahead to say, *"Luxury and sloth led easily and naturally to lust."*

Let me give you the factors of Joseph's victory as Brother Sanders goes ahead to write:

> *He was strengthened by the fact that his praiseworthy loyalty to his master was exceeded by his loyalty to God.*
>
> *To him a sin against God was immeasurable more serious than a crime against man. To him the essence of sin was that it was against God.*
>
> *He retained the capacity of being shacked by sin.*
>
> *His mind was not conditioned for a fall.*

Here I believe more fall than anywhere else. Joseph's mind was always on a preparatory stage of resistance against sin. His mind was set not to sin; what about yours? Sometimes people just want to sin in the flesh but cannot at times find a legal way to commit it. When in time the enemy sets up a trap for them to feel they cannot help themselves, since their mind is ready to do it, the opportunity is all that this mind needed. Expression of the imagination is either sinful or righteous.

Samson was a man of God who had fallen into sin one time too many. Yet he would repent and turn back to God. His great fall was that he was tempted to take the grace and anointing of the Lord further than he was supposed to. As a Nazarite, he broke his vows to God, controlled by his uncontrolled lustful desire for love and pleasure; fulfilling all his flesh wanted, he drowned in lust and was lost.

"He fought in vengeance for the wrong done against him, than for the cause of his land and people."

Believer, don't tempt God by playing with sin, fulfilling your fleshly desires and expect the anointing of God to show up on you when needed. As someone has said, "Whoever has God knows it; whomsoever He has left knows it not."

"Grace is given freely, yet you should keep receiving it every morning to keep an overflow, living on yesterday's grace will make you run out of it soon."

Let me add for your edification these passages from the Word:

> He who, being often reproved, hardens his neck shall suddenly be destroyed—and that without remedy. (Proverbs 29:1)

> Everything is permissible (allowable and lawful) for me; but not all things are helpful (good for me to do, expedient and profitable when considered with other things). Everything is lawful for me, but I will not become the slave of anything *or* be brought under its power.

> Food [is intended] for the stomach and the stomach for food, but God will finally end [the functions of] both *and* bring them to nothing. The body is not intended for sexual immorality, but [is intended] for the Lord, and the Lord [is intended] for the body [to save, sanctify, and raise it again].

And God both raised the Lord to life and will also raise us up by His power.

Do you not see *and* know that your bodies are members (bodily parts) of Christ (the Messiah)? Am I therefore to take the parts of Christ and make [them] parts of a prostitute? Never! Never!

Or do you not know *and* realize that when a man joins himself to a prostitute, he becomes one body with her? The two, it is written, shall become one flesh.

But the person who is united to the Lord becomes one spirit with Him.

Shun immorality *and* all sexual looseness [flee from impurity in thought, word, or deed]. Any other sin which a man commits is one outside the body, but he who commits sexual immorality sins against his own body.

Do you not know that your body is the temple (the very sanctuary) of the Holy Spirit Who lives within you, whom you have received [as a Gift] from God? You are not your own,

You were bought with a price [purchased with preciousness and paid for, made His own]. So then, honor God *and* bring glory to Him in your body. (1 Corinthians 6:12–20)

Let's look at one more scripture before we break down this passage and see what the Lord is saying to us.

> Do you not discern *and* understand that you
> [the whole church at Corinth] are God's temple
> (His sanctuary), and that God's Spirit has His
> permanent dwelling in you [to be at home in you,
> collectively as a church and also individually]?

> If anyone does hurt to God's temple *or* corrupts
> it [with false doctrines] *or* destroys it, God will
> do hurt to him *and* bring him to the corruption
> of death *and* destroy him. For the temple of God
> is holy (sacred to Him) and that [temple] you [the
> believing church and its individual believers] are.
> (1 Corinthians 3:16–17)

Most times, when you speak to correct someone concerning the improper wearing of clothing, the reply sounds something like this: "My body, my pleasure"; "I will do what I *feel* is right to do." Now put these two statements in contrast with the scriptures that you have just read. As a child of God, it's no more your body; you have been rightfully bought by Redemption. You were God's before sin, and after your faith in Jesus, you have become His again. Church, this truth needs to get into the believer's heart: "I am just a steward of His body, and I will have to give an account for everything wrong that I do to His body."

God takes desire in His prized possession. He has cleansed and made our spirit man new from sin. Our soul—mind, will, and emotions—are in the process of being saved, but our bodies cry out for salvation, for redemption. Jesus on the cross offered His body and was broken and bruised that yours and mine might receive salvation from the effects of sin. His head was crowned with thorns so that it would be possible for the born-again believer of Jesus to receive the mind of Christ.

The Lord is for the body, and your body is for the Lord. Now you cannot take what is God's and pollute it with something other than what God has assigned it for, as it is a serious business for the body which is God's dwelling place here on earth. Let me give you a scripture that makes God's claim official.

> In Him you also who have heard the Word of Truth, the glad tidings (Gospel) of your salvation, and have believed in *and* adhered to *and* relied on Him, were stamped with the seal of the long-promised Holy Spirit.
>
> That [Spirit] is the guarantee of our inheritance [the first fruits, the pledge and foretaste, the down payment on our heritage], in anticipation of its full redemption *and* our acquiring [complete] possession of it—to the praise of His glory. (Ephesians 1:13–14)

On the day of Redemption, when God is returning to take back His property, you will have to give an account of what you did with His body. It does seriously matter what you do with your bodies as believers. God paid a high price to buy it back from the effects of sin and the Devil. Don't you realize that that's the very reason believers bury their dead rather than cremating them? Why do you think the spirits of the dead will go back into the grave and resurrect us with our bodies? And those who are alive shall be changed with their bodies.

Jesus could have left His body in the grave and appeared to His disciples in a spirit form as angels do. Yet He rose from the death with His resurrected body. Jesus took care of His body and even told His disciples to rest at times and take care of themselves.

Note carefully: your body and the desires of the flesh are two different things. Your body does what your mind and spirit tells it to do. Whatever you train your body to do, that shall it do. Just as you program a robot to a set memory, it will simply follow out what is put in there.

Flesh is a set pattern of thinking and so are its evil desires that are against the will and purpose of God. Take control of what you let through your eyes and ears. This affects your thinking, which in turn affects what you will do with your body, whether you offer it to God as a living sacrifice or offer it to sin and all unrighteousness.

As I sat studying on holiness, the Spirit of God one day opened my eyes to the following scriptures that I believe will greatly bless you all.

> I appeal to you therefore, brethren, *and* beg of you in view of [all] the mercies of God, to make a decisive dedication of your bodies [presenting all your members and faculties] as a living sacrifice, holy (devoted, consecrated) and well pleasing to God, which is your reasonable (rational, intelligent) service *and* spiritual worship. (Romans 12:1)

All that the Lord by His spirit was revealing to Paul was the need to *be holy; set apart in his body only for God, and serve only God.* The sacrifices in biblical terms had to be kept apart from the rest of the group to be completely *holy;* they had to be separated and taken care of as the family's loved one, and much time and effort were spent on it. It was separated to God, it was *holy* to God, and it could not have defects on it.

A living sacrifice, acceptable in the sight of God, is one who is holy unto God, to God *alone.* We are His, so let us continue to offer ourselves to Him as a living sacrifice, holy and pleasing to God, separated from worldly thinking and beliefs to Bible-believing.

Please read this scripture:

> You offspring of vipers! How can you speak good things when you are evil (wicked)? For out of the fullness (the overflow, the superabundance) of the heart the mouth speaks.
>
> The good man from his inner good treasure flings forth good things, and the evil man out of his inner evil storehouse flings forth evil things. (Matthew 12:34–35)

Now you see the word from your mouth is the expression of your heart (spirit). If you desire to change the produce of the tree, you will need to change the whole tree, and a totally new tree has to be created in your inner spirit.

> For we are God's [own] handiwork (His workmanship), recreated in Christ Jesus, [born anew] that we may do those good works which God predestined (planned beforehand) for us [taking paths which He prepared ahead of time], that we should walk in them [living the good life which He prearranged and made ready for us to live]. (Ephesians 2:10)

This you also do with your mouth as you confess the Lordship of Jesus in your life and eternity. If you speak out of the overflow of the heart, it is important to know where our heart gets its overflow from. To get something to overflow, it needs to keep receiving.

> Keep *and* guard your heart with all vigilance *and* above all that you guard, for out of it flow the springs of life. (Proverbs 4:23)

Now you realize it's in your heart that you are declared clean or unclean. "Brother Bryan, how do I guard my heart?" *Simply by guarding the entrance.* Your mouth gate, your eye gate and your ear gate—these feed your soul with either the life-giving Word or the fear and sorrow of the world. The choice of what you see and what you hear does affect what you speak. Words create images, and that image is what you go out each day to follow.

Think about the story of the Tower of Babel, where God confounded the language. The people had imagined to build a tower in self-effort to reach heaven. So they went out to pursue that till God came into the scene and set everything in order. Therefore, child of God, I encourage you to guard your heart by guarding the entrance to your heart. Watch what you allow through your eyes, watch what you allow through your ears, and watch what you're speaking.

If you have guarded the entrances to your heart, then you have very well guarded your heart.

> Do not fret *or* have any anxiety about anything, but in every circumstance *and* in everything, by prayer and petition (definite requests), with thanksgiving, continue to make your wants known to God.
>
> And God's peace [shall be yours, that tranquil state of a soul assured of its salvation through Christ, and so fearing nothing from God and being content with its earthly lot of whatever sort that is, that peace] which transcends all understanding shall garrison *and* mount guard over your hearts and minds in Christ Jesus. (Philippians 4:6–7)

You will notice here that when you have prayed with a definite petition to the Father on the matter of your weakness or trouble—even the good things of life—the peace of God *garrisons* or guards your heart and soul from outside influences. This is when you are not going to be troubled about many things, since the most important thing you have chosen is the Word of Christ.

I have learned that thoughts are eternal and don't die. Therefore don't put images and open your ears to error, doubts, or disputing, for that will create thoughts that will work against you rather than for you. You may be wondering then about the thoughts that are wrong and already inside you. Relax; there is always a way out. The only way you can overcome negative and fearful, sinful thought is by *overloading* your eyes and ears with God's words and with messages that exalt Jesus and bring answers rather than creating troubles. It does not mean you do not have that wrong thought in you, but by the time you go looking for it, you will have to go thought a thousand faith words before you find that one fear thought. By the time you move to even feel or think that fear, faith will suppress it—just the way fear suppressed faith before.

Let me end this chapter by saying *what you behold is what you will eventually become.* Everything is first translated before it can be put to use in us. Just as with food, we don't eat vitamin C from oranges; we drink orange juice which gives us vitamin C. In the same way, what you put through your eyes and ears will be translated into thoughts and manifested through issues in life in both the physical and spiritual realms.

CHAPTER 8

The Grace of God

I could never understand the power of righteousness till I understood the power of God's grace. *Everything that God gives us is through grace, and we receive His grace through the act of faith.*

> Therefore, [inheriting] the promise is the outcome of faith *and* depends [entirely] on faith, in order that it might be given as an act of grace (unmerited favor), to make it stable *and* valid *and* guaranteed to all his descendants—not only to the devotees *and* adherents of the Law, but also to those who share the faith of Abraham, who is [thus] the father of us all. (Romans 4:16)

People often tell new believers more about the power of sin and its ability to destroy than grace's ability to protect and strengthen. Church, if you understand the grace of God for your life, sinning against God will never be your problem.

> But then Law came in, [only] to expand *and* increase the trespass [making it more apparent and exciting opposition]. But where sin increased *and* abounded, grace (God's unmerited favor) has surpassed it *and* increased the more *and* superabounded ... (Romans 5:20)

Grace is and always will be greater and stronger than sin and its power over our lives.

> But God's free gift is not at all to be compared to the trespass [His grace is out of all proportion to the fall of man]. For if many died through one man's falling away (his lapse, his offense), much more profusely did God's grace and the free gift [that comes] through the undeserved favor of the one Man Jesus Christ abound *and* overflow to *and* for [the benefit of] many.

> For if because of one man's trespass (lapse, offense) death reigned through that one, much more surely will those who receive [God's] overflowing grace (unmerited favor) and the free gift of righteousness [putting them into right standing with Himself] reign as kings in life through the one Man Jesus Christ (the Messiah, the Anointed One). (Romans 5:15, 17)

I was struggling with the power of sin, since that was all I was used to and how I was brought up to deal with sin (disobedience to the commandments of God). The day the Lord showed me that *My grace is all you need for all the victories that you will ever seek in your life,* my struggle was over, sin and condemnation ceased, and I am no longer the same.

The power of grace can only be realized and experienced in its fullness in our lives when *we receive it by faith and not by our keeping the commandments.* Let's look at some more scriptures in the light of the free, undeserved grace we have received and enjoy today.

> Even when we were dead (slain) by [our own] shortcomings *and* trespasses, He made us alive

together in fellowship *and* in union with Christ; [He gave us the very life of Christ Himself, the same new life with which He quickened Him, for] it is by grace (His favor and mercy which you did not deserve) that you are saved (delivered from judgment and made partakers of Christ's salvation).

He did this that He might clearly demonstrate through the ages to come the immeasurable (limitless, surpassing) riches of His free grace (His unmerited favor) in [His] kindness *and* goodness of heart toward us in Christ Jesus.

For it is by free grace (God's unmerited favor) that you are saved (delivered from judgment *and* made partakers of Christ's salvation) through [your] faith. And this [salvation] is not of yourselves [of your own doing, it came not through your own striving], but it is the gift of God ... (Ephesians 2:5, 7–8)

Thank God for being gracious to us and saving us. It is still through grace that He saves us. Do not take too much pride in how many Scripture verses you know or how long you have been in church; what really matters is Amazing Grace. Learn the love the Father has for you, and don't try to talk about your love for the Father. It is He who first loved us and gave Himself in Jesus to us, long before we ever knew or loved Him. The words used to describe the grace of God toward us in Christ include *immeasurable, limitless, surpassing riches*, and above all *free*, which truly sums it up: *free. Just for the by faith receive.*

I do understand that many trifle with the grace of God and sin, thinking that they will get with it, but they are living in a complete deception. The grace of God is more than we could ever understand, yet since God is also the God of justice, He will not just let sin go unchecked. He has pronounced His curse on sin from the beginning, saying, "Whosoever sins shall die." Get under the blood flow, and you will be all right. Don't try to twist Scripture to satisfy carnal desires; let the Scriptures speak and you follow.

> For the wages which sin pays is death, but the [bountiful] free gift of God is eternal life through (in union with) Jesus Christ our Lord. (Romans 6:23)

When we work, we receive wages; it works the same way with sin. When we sin, we are bound to receive wages for sinning. Sin pays its workers in full; it's just the timing and method of payment that differ. Some receive their wages in installments, some one time in full, and others receive it in pension form. But you are sure to receive the penalty for sin. David was forgiven for his acts of murder and adultery, yet the Bible says that the sword never left his house.

> Then note *and* appreciate the gracious kindness and the severity of God: severity toward those who have fallen, but God's gracious kindness to you— provided you continue in His grace *and* abide in His kindness; otherwise you too will be cut off (pruned away). (Romans 11:22)

Grace does not give anyone the license to sin, though rightly understood and appropriated, it will bring many blessings and victories. God's grace will keep you from sin, for grace is a person, Jesus. You will need to see yourself in the finished work of Jesus; you will not go through as David had to, since you have the advantage of being one with Jesus.

> And God is able to make all grace (every favor and earthly blessing] come to you in abundance, so that you may always *and* under all circumstances *and*

> whatever the need be self-sufficient [possessing enough to require no aid or support and furnished in abundance for every good work and charitable donation]. (2 Corinthians 9:8)

When the grace of God is in control of our life, we have no problem. Those who fully understand and are living daily by the power of the grace of God know exactly what power there is to overcome and fight off every temptation and attack of the Devil.

Paul struggled with a messenger of Satan, probably a human who continuously troubled and withstood him nearly everywhere he went to preach. Such a one would remind Paul of his past and bring fights and divisions where Paul had just preached peace and love. When he went to God with his need, this was God's answer: "My grace is enough for all your tests and trials." You see that His grace is all we need today. *Grace, grace ...* say it again: *Grace, grace.*

> But He said to me, My grace (My favor and loving-kindness and mercy) is enough for you [sufficient against any danger and enables you to bear the trouble manfully]; for *My* strength *and* power are made perfect (fulfilled and completed) *and show themselves most effective* in [your] weakness. Therefore, I will all the more gladly glory in my weaknesses *and* infirmities, that the strength *and* power of Christ (the Messiah) may rest (yes, may pitch a tent over and dwell) upon me! (2 Corinthians 12:9)

His strength made strong in weakness is God's grace. As you are faced with many types of temptations, remember that His grace is yours now. His favor is upon you because of what Jesus has done, not what we do.

Let's look at this scripture and see how grace helps us in overcoming temptations.

> But He gives us more and more grace (power of the Holy Spirit, to meet this evil tendency and all others fully). That is why He says, God sets Himself against the proud and haughty, but gives grace [continually] to the lowly (those who are humble enough to receive it). (James 4:6)

I have seen that, as you seek the grace of God daily as your daily bread, you will find mercy and the favor of God in all your ways.

By the Spirit of God, James said that grace is God's empowerment upon us sinners made righteous to stay righteous and to overcome all evil tendencies of our life by the grace and love of our Lord Jesus.

> Let us then fearlessly *and* confidently *and* boldly draw near to the throne of grace (the throne of God's unmerited favor to us sinners), that we may receive mercy [for our failures] and find grace to help in good time for every need [appropriate help and well-timed help, coming just when we need it]. (Hebrews 4:16)

Church, it is time. Let us move on from that so-called manhood which thinks it has everything under control, when it has nothing. It is time to fall on our knees and call on God to have mercy and give grace for each day as fresh bread.

Believer, it is time to humble yourself under the mighty hand of God and ask for His help. We have come to think that humbling is a weak thing, but rather it is the place where a believer finds grace and receives mercy, coming on time as we need it.

> For who are you, O great mountain [of human obstacles]? Before Zerubbabel [who with Joshua had led the return of the exiles from Babylon and was undertaking the rebuilding of the temple, before him] you shall become a plain [a mere molehill]! And he shall bring forth the finishing gable stone [of the new temple] with loud shoutings of the people, crying, Grace, grace to it! (Zechariah 4:7)

Look at what God says will bring down even the greatest mountain in life, the shouting cry of "Grace." If you are facing a mountain of temptations, shout it out and shout it loud: *Lord, I speak grace! Grace! over my situations, and I know they shall be removed in Jesus' name.*

Sometimes we need to shout out what we really believe and what we stand for; it does release the power of God on our behalf.

Living with grace shows God that you cannot do it and you are calling God to attention that if He does not do it, it shall not be done any other way. *It's either God's way or no way.*

> So get rid of all uncleanness and the rampant outgrowth of wickedness, and in a humble (gentle, modest) spirit receive *and* welcome the Word, which implanted *and* rooted [in your hearts] contains the power to save your souls. (James 1:21)

Grace flows where the Word of God flows. It will save your soul, and a new person will rise in the power of the Spirit. While we are on the topic of grace, we need to keep this scripture handy in connection with temptation:

> For the grace of God (His unmerited favor and blessing) has come forward (appeared) for the

deliverance from sin *and* the eternal salvation for all mankind.

It has trained us to reject *and* renounce all ungodliness (irreligion) and worldly (passionate) desires, to live discreet (temperate, self-controlled), upright, devout (spiritually whole) lives in this present world,

Awaiting *and* looking for the [fulfillment, the realization of our] blessed hope, even the glorious appearing of our great God and Savior Christ Jesus (the Messiah, the Anointed One) ... (Titus 2:11–13)

Here you will see what most extreme grace preachers don't want to touch in regard to temptation: *grace appeared for the deliverance **from sin, not to sin***. We are to renounce all ungodliness and worldly passions, yet what has happened with grace is that people with their desire for pleasure have used God's grace and love as an excuse to remain in the pleasures of the world and ungodly behavior. They speak of this as natural problems, when it is spiritual disobedience to the power of grace that can set them free, now.

Some have said we are free from works, yet we are *free from dead works, not free from doing good works*. We still are doing good, like our heavenly Father and our Lord Jesus, who went about doing good and healing all who were oppressed of the Devil.

The church of Jesus has to be founded in the full revelation of the finished work of Jesus on the cross to the throne. Yet this does not mean we are in any way to be tossed around by every wind of doctrine, coming through any means which goes against the Word of God and His revealed purposes.

CHAPTER 9

God is a Good God

I am reminded of Oral Roberts in his early years of ministry when he stated boldly on television that "something good is going to happen to you." Church people were violently against the thought that one could expect good from God, even by faith. One reason was low self-esteem, when in fact the blood of Jesus has made us righteous and given us the power to call God Father. Which good father does not want his children to have the best every day when he has the power to make that good?

Many have blamed God for all the bad things that happen on earth and in people's lives. I would like to finish by clearing the air with the truth of God, as if He tests and tries us with evil.

> O give thanks to the Lord, for He is good; for
> His mercy *and* loving-kindness endure forever.
> (Psalm 136:1)

You see here how clearly this scripture says that *God is good*. He can only be one thing, not both. He is good. So why do we go and say that He is not good, by saying that "God put this trouble on me to test me"? No, He does not.

> If you then, evil as you are, know how to give good
> *and* advantageous gifts to your children, how much
> more will your Father Who is in heaven [perfect as

He is] give good *and* advantageous things to those
who keep on asking Him! (Matthew 7:11)

God is perfect and good. He will give us goodness and good
things for our advantage. So why do you want to make God a
child abuser, by saying, "God put this sickness and pain on me"?
He is a good Father, and he will never do that.

We often hear the story of Job and want to prove a point from
his life. Realize that he lived before Christ and His provisions of
healing, when people were declared righteous or guilty by their
actions. In the case of Job, God was not sending him pain and
trouble. It was Job who allowed the fear of his life to take effect.
As much as the just shall live by their faith, those in fear will
have fear to live by.

And when the days of their feasting were over,
Job sent for them to purify *and* hallow them, and
rose up early in the morning and offered burnt
offerings according to the number of them all. For
Job said, It may be that my sons have sinned and
cursed *or* disowned God in their hearts. Thus did
Job at all [such] times. (Job 1:5)

For the thing which I greatly fear comes upon me,
and that of which I am afraid befalls me. (Job 3:25)

What befell him was what he kept on fearing. No wonder every
time the children had a celebration, the next morning Job was
sacrificing in fear of disaster. He too believed that God had a
stick and was ready to punish all disobedience with evil. No;
God is a good God. Adam made the same mistake of fearing that
God was trying to keep good from them. Today we ask whether
God's Word might not prove out as true. *To fear God's Word is to
distrust God Himself. God is not a man, that He should lie.*

If God kept records and punished us for the sins we committed, then we would have been punished properly till we had learned the lesson. But there is forgiveness with You, O Lord, that You may be feared. O give thanks to the Lord, for He is good, and His mercy and loving-kindness endure forever.

> Let no one say when he is tempted, I am tempted from God; for God is incapable of being tempted by [what is] evil and He Himself tempts no one.
>
> But every person is tempted when he is drawn away, enticed *and* baited by his own evil desire (lust, passions).
>
> Then the evil desire, when it has conceived, gives birth to sin, and sin, when it is fully matured, brings forth death.
>
> Do not be misled, my beloved brethren.
>
> Every good gift and every perfect (free, large, full) gift is from above; it comes down from the Father of all [that gives] light, in [the shining of] Whom there can be no variation [rising or setting] or shadow cast by His turning [as in an eclipse]. (James 1:13–17)

Now, after reading this letter God allowed James to write, do we see that God cannot be tempted by our evil selfish motives, nor does He tempt anyone? He cannot tempt or test you with anything evil or bad. Such trials all come because we do not guard our heart by guarding our mouth, and there you have all you said. Life and death are in the power of the tongue, and they that love it shall eat the fruits of it. By speaking out of wrong information, you can do more harm to yourself than good—and then multiply the wrong by blaming God for that.

Look at this scripture and see for yourself that God is doing everything to deliver you from temptation and not give you one.

> For no temptation (no trial regarded as enticing to sin), [no matter how it comes or where it leads] has overtaken you *and* laid hold on you that is not common to man [that is, no temptation or trial has come to you that is beyond human resistance and that is not adjusted and adapted and belonging to human experience, and such as man can bear]. But God is faithful [to His Word and to His compassionate nature], and He [can be trusted] not to let you be tempted *and* tried *and* assayed beyond your ability *and* strength of resistance *and* power to endure, but with the temptation He will [always] also provide the way out (the means of escape to a landing place), that you may be capable *and* strong *and* powerful to bear up under it patiently. (1 Corinthians 10:13)

One more very important point is to know that God will never allow the devil to test or try you with a test that you cannot pass and that God is faithful to make a way of escape even in your temptations. He will never allow you to go through more than you have the knowledge and grace to overcome and win every time in Jesus' name.

Child of God, let me show you this scripture, though you may have seen it many times.

> Surely *or* only goodness, mercy, *and* unfailing love shall follow me all the days of my life, and through the length of my days the house of the Lord [and His presence] shall be my dwelling place. (Psalm 23:6)

Do you see the benefits of staying in your Father's house? Surely good things and mercy and favor follow me all the days of my life here on earth.

We could go on, but I believe that once you receive the gift of righteousness and abundance of grace, you will never have to worry about being brought down by any temptation at all. God is faithful; He will protect and preserve you blameless till the coming of our Lord Jesus Christ.

Rejoice and declare, "I am free! I am free in Jesus' name! And *something good happens to me every day of my life, for I live by faith, and I let the good Shepherd, Jesus, lead me all the way through.*

Every temptation has this point in common, stressing that God does not love me enough. Therefore many times believers go into establishing their own efforts at pleasing God. This is wrong, because *God loves you!* Adam thought that, and ever since he did, humankind tends to think, *Maybe I have to be good enough for God to do something for me.* Remember it's not because of your goodness that God is good; it's because God is good in the first place that he is good to you and me. In Jesus, our Savior, God is already pleased with us, since I am in Him, and He is in me.

Knowing and experiencing God's goodness leads people to repentance, just as Zacchaeus experienced:

> So then Zacchaeus stood up and solemnly declared to the Lord, See, Lord, the half of my goods I [now] give [by way of restoration] to the poor, and if I have cheated anyone out of anything, I [now] restore four times as much.

> And Jesus said to him, Today is Messianic and spiritual] salvation come to [all the members of]

this household, since Zacchaeus too is a [real spiritual] son of Abraham. (Luke 19:8–9)

Jesus did not teach him before he did this; Jesus loved him and bestowed His goodness of being on his house, when others said otherwise.

The goodness of God causes change, but if you are the same or even become worse and say, "God understands, and this is His grace," then that is foolishness. If you have experienced God's goodness for even a moment, you will be changed. The love of God changes even the worst of sinners, but becoming responsive to carnal and fleshly desires rather than what the Word says will cause much pain and error of faith in one's life.

CHAPTER 10

The Sense of Righteousness

Let me end here by giving you a peaceful thought that the Lord Jesus wants you to have: You can of your own do nothing. Let Jesus lead you, and simply live in the righteousness He has died to provide for you. When you know your standing in Christ, you will live the rest of your abundant life from that position of provision. To be conscious of righteousness and walk your entire earthly life on the finished work of Jesus is miraculous.

> Let not sin therefore rule as king in your mortal (short-lived, perishable) bodies, to make you yield to its cravings *and* be subject to its lusts *and* evil passions.
>
> Do not continue offering or yielding your bodily members [and faculties] to sin as instruments (tools) of wickedness. But offer *and* yield yourselves to God as though you have been raised from the dead to [perpetual] life, and your bodily members [and faculties] to God, presenting them as implements of righteousness.
>
> And having been set free from sin, you have become the servants of righteousness (of conformity to the divine will in thought, purpose, and action).

I am speaking in familiar human terms because of your natural limitations. For as you yielded your bodily members [and faculties] as servants to impurity and ever increasing lawlessness, so now yield your bodily members [and faculties] once for all as servants to righteousness (right being and doing) [which leads] to sanctification. (Romans 6:12–13, 18–19)

There we have it: we yield to the power of righteousness rather than the power of sin. Jesus is made unto us righteousness. You may say, "How can that be, since we are all sinners?" Wait a minute; we *were* sinners, but we have been saved by Jesus, given His righteousness, and declared by Him as righteous in God's eyes. Now you cannot be double-minded. You must make up your mind whether you are a sinner or a saved believer who has been made righteous.

God's great love toward us has been so strong that He had grace on us and Himself paid the price for our deliverance from sin. He asked only that we should believe on the Son, Jesus, and receive His finished work as our access to God the Father's throne, to be seated with Christ on the right hand of God.

For our sake He made Christ [virtually] to be sin Who knew no sin, so that in *and* through Him we might become [endued with, viewed as being in, and examples of] the righteousness of God [what we ought to be, approved and acceptable and in right relationship with Him, by His goodness]. (2 Corinthians 5:21)

He became sin, and by faith's divine exchange, we become righteous. What a miracle of God's love toward us. People have lived all their lives in condemnation, guilt, shame, and sin consciousness. All that has brought nothing but pain and fear.

What Jesus did is far more than remove sin; He put us in the *"garden of Eden, standing" before the Father.* Recall how Adam felt about God and how they talked openly. There was nothing that the man Adam could not do. He was aware of being righteous, and this helped him talk with God and live long. Righteousness makes you pray bold, strong prayers like Elijah did. Your boldness can be compared to a lion when you stand on your Christ-bestowed righteousness.

Child of God, receive today what Jesus has done for you, and by faith confess that over your life. Then see the power of righteousness work its work in you. When we awake to the reality of righteousness that Jesus has provided, then sin will no longer have any place in us.

Our new identity is Jesus. He is all we need, and His Word is all we spiritually eat by reading and meditating and confessing it. Continue your path of righteousness faithfully and consistently, and you will experience the original plan of God for life and overcome every temptation that comes your way.

May Jesus, our good Shepherd, guide you all the way as you choose to walk by faith, and work by looking at the Master. Jesus is easy; religion is hard. Stand fast in the liberty wherewith Christ has made you free, and do not be entangled in temptation again.

<u>Contact the Author</u>

Bryan Prasad
P.O. Box 3762
Samabula, Fiji Islands
+679 – 996 – 6054
bryanap@connect.com.fj
jclm@live.com